# Meals to Remember

*A Celebration of Duck*

# Meals to Remember

*A Celebration of Duck*

Maple Leaf Farms®

**FRP.**

**Favorite Recipes® Press**

Copyright © 2008 by
Maple Leaf Farms, Inc.
9166 North 200 East
Milford, IN 46542
574-658-4121
www.mapleleaffarms.com

Library of Congress Control Number: 2008923881
ISBN: 978-0-9801968-0-1

Favorite Recipes Press is an imprint of FRP, Inc.,
a wholly owned subsidiary of Southwestern/Great American, Inc.
P.O. Box 305142
Nashville, Tennessee 37230
800-358-0560

Art Direction: Steve Newman
Book Design: David Malone
Project Editor: Susan Larson
Project Coordinator: Tanis Westbrook

Manufactured in the United States of America
First Printing 2008  12,500 copies

*This book is dedicated to the memory of
Donald Wentzel. His desire for excellence and
innovation remains a hallmark at the company he
founded in 1958. His foresight, dedication, and
vision set the foundation for Maple Leaf Farms,
which stands today as his living legacy.*

## Acknowledgments

Photography
Rex Harrell
Richard Spahr
Tim Turner
Kirsty Saalfrank
Barb Coad

Wine Selections
Efrain Madrigal

Menus and Recipes
Karen Levin
Caren Messina-Hirsch
The Tucker Family

Maple Leaf Farms
Karen Clark
Darla Gagnon
Nora Macon
Jodi Richcreek
Scott Swaidner
Chris Zielasko

Coordination
Melinda Mains

# Meals to Remember

*A Celebration of Duck*

Chinese New Year

Valentine's Day

Cocktail Party

Family Reunion

Luau

Picnic on the Beach

Mountaintop Brunch

Sunset Cruise

# Meals to Remember

*A Celebration of Duck*

Mexican Birthday

Garden Party

Fourth of July

Tailgating

Thanksgiving

Holiday Party

# Maple Leaf Farms Celebrates Fifty years of Quality

It's no accident that Maple Leaf Farms is the nation's leading duck producer. In 1958, when Donald Wentzel bought a small duck farm in Milford, Indiana, he founded the company on quality— "Quality you can count on." He believed that production control would yield excellent quality.

*Don Wentzel,*
*Founder of Maple Leaf Farms*

Wentzel spent more than twenty years working in the grain industry. As a national sales manager for Chicago-based Hales & Hunter feed company, he became familiar with the Long Island duck industry. Although he thought duck was very tasty and it had the potential to grow in popularity, he saw some inherent business challenges for duck production in that region—namely, the high cost of shipping in grain to feed the ducks and the cost associated with shipping the product to markets outside of the Northeast. It made much more sense to him to raise ducks in the Midwest, where feed ingredients were readily available and growing markets across the country could be easily serviced.

Independent at heart, Wentzel and his wife, Myrtle, decided to strike out on their own. After a brief stint at row crop production, they founded Wentzel Feed Company in Mentone, Indiana, to distribute feeds directly to farmers. As they began this business, Wentzel also decided to try his hand at producing commercial ducks. He and some family friends began raising ducks on their family farms. They hauled them to Michigan to be processed.

*Myrtle and Don Wentzel along with daughter Sandra sit down for a holiday feast of duck.*

"Quality you can count on."

*Don Wentzel and Terry Tucker inspect a duck in the early 1960s.*

When this processing plant closed, Wentzel decided to establish his own company. A Milford, Indiana, poultry farm and its accompanying processing plant came up for sale. So he purchased it, intent on making sure that high quality duck would become more available. With this move, Maple Leaf Farms was born.

Wentzel relied on good friends to help him launch his business. Myrtle's brother-in-law, Joe Boggs, and other friends who had been raising ducks with Wentzel before he formed the company continued growing ducks on their farms. And he asked his colleague from Hales & Hunter, Clarence "Brick" Meinert, to join him in his new venture. When the demand for duck increased, Brick began to raise ducks on his own farm and talked his brother, Al Meinert, into raising ducks to help meet the need.

Brick Meinert was officially Maple Leaf Farms' "employee number one." Meinert was the first plant manager, but had responsibilities in many other areas of the company's operations. He and Wentzel worked hand-in-hand in the early years to grow the business, complementing each other's abilities and accepting new challenges along the way.

That first year Maple Leaf Farms raised approximately 280,000 ducks. It marketed almost twice that many ducks the following year. By 1964, the company was producing one million ducks a year. Always focused on quality, Wentzel nurtured the growth of his business until his death in 1968.

After Wentzel's passing, his son-in-law, Terry Tucker, took the helm. Tucker was a longtime employee. In the mid-1950s, he had begun working part-time on Wentzel's duck farm during high school. While working at the farm, he met Wentzel's pretty young daughter, Sandra. The two hit it off and were wed four years later, while Tucker was studying agricultural economics at Purdue University. After he graduated, Tucker joined Maple Leaf Farms and began helping Wentzel and others manage various aspects of the business.

Under Tucker's leadership, Maple Leaf Farms established itself as the leader of the duck industry by moving toward a vertically integrated organization. He saw that the company could more easily fulfill Wentzel's mission of producing high quality duck products if it directly controlled and linked the many operations that affected quality. As a result, he oversaw the construction and purchase of a number of key facilities.

*Don Wentzel — late 1950s*

Today, Maple Leaf Farms remains a family-owned and operated company. Terry has passed the torch to the third generation. His sons, John and Scott Tucker, serve as the company's co-presidents, and his daughter, Tricia Tucker Rice, serves on the Board of Directors. Together the Tucker family has continued Donald Wentzel's vision of producing high quality duck products.

## A Fifty-Year Recipe for Success

With a foundation of quality, Maple Leaf Farms built on its early success by becoming more involved with each step of production through vertical integration. By developing a network of vertically integrated operations, the company could control each step of the production process and create duck products with superior quality and consistency. This became Maple Leaf Farms' recipe for success.

When Terry Tucker began leading the company, Maple Leaf Farms made several moves to grow and integrate its business by expanding its operations, including building one feed mill and purchasing another, which allowed the company to produce its own high quality feeds. The company also broadened operations with new hatcheries, a diagnostics laboratory, a prepared foods plant, and feather processing facilities. In the late 1970s, it extended its product line to include other poultry products.

In 1981, Maple Leaf Farms acquired its largest competitor, C&D Foods of Wisconsin, a duck industry giant with extensive research capabilities. This acquisition allowed the company to become a major competitor in the duck industry and begin many extensive research and breeding programs.

The late 1990s marked another period of significant growth for Maple Leaf Farms. During this time, the company constructed a new distribution center and a new biosecure breeding farm. The company also expanded its operations by purchasing Woodland Farms, a California-based company serving Asian markets across the West Coast. These moves solidified Maple Leaf's position as North America's leading duck producer.

Despite its tremendous growth, Maple Leaf Farms has not lost sight of the values that its founder, Donald Wentzel, held dear. It continues to be a company committed to family, community, and quality—key ingredients to success.

*Today Maple Leaf Farms is owned and operated by the Tucker family.*

*Terry Tucker, CEO, and sons John and Scott, co-presidents, manage the company.*

*Brick Meinert (Maple Leaf Farms' first employee) barbecues duck for the employees.*

## The Meals You'll Remember
## Start with Maple Leaf Farms Duck

Maple Leaf Farms duck products are known for their exceptional quality and dependable consistency. Restaurant operators throughout North America rely on our products to help them meet and exceed the expectations of their customers. One taste of our quality duck products and you'll see why Maple Leaf Farms has been one of America's most respected food suppliers for fifty years.

And we are still improving our duck. Through innovative natural breeding and feeding programs, our duck is 27 percent leaner than fifteen years ago. In fact, a serving of our skinless duck breast is actually lower in fat and calories than a comparable serving of chicken.

In addition to being a healthy alternative to other meat and poultry, duck is very versatile. Our line of duck products includes fresh or frozen whole duck and boneless duck breasts that can be used for a variety of exciting duck meals. And our fully cooked roast half duck, which has been a flagship product for twenty years, is heat-and-serve, which allows chefs and consumers alike the chance to easily create their own dishes with our tender, flavorful duck.

To build on the success of these foods, new and exciting duck products are continually in the works at Maple Leaf Farms' research and development kitchen. There our corporate chefs develop innovative products and recipes that meet the needs of our customers. In recent years, we have extended our line of convenient duck products to include easy-to-prepare items like our rotisserie duck breasts and halves, a full line of gourmet, flavor-marinated duck breasts, duck sausage, duck leg confit, and a microwavable grilled duck breast.

Although culinary trends and consumers' tastes have shifted over the years, Maple Leaf Farms duck has remained a constant for folks who seek to create memorable meals.

*Maple Leaf Farms*
*Celebrates Fifty Years of Quality*

I like using Maple Leaf duck products because of their consistent product and freshness. I have used them for many years and have not had one issue with anything. It is by far a superior product.

Bill Alt — *Executive Chef*
Kincaids Fish, Chop and Steakhouse, *Bloomington, Minnesota*

*"Love the duck!" "Tender and juicy." "Best duck I've ever had!" These are a few of the many great comments from our guests after enjoying the Maple Leaf Farms duck breast at our restaurant. Keep those happy ducks coming our way!!*

Billy Quon — *Owner*    Herbert Amaya — *Executive Chef*
Volcano Grill, *Carmel Valley, CA*

*There is always a place on my menu for Maple Leaf Farms duck. I have long referred to my style of cooking as "food with integrity," and Maple Leaf products live up to that description.*

Ted Cizma — *Executive Chef*
Grand Traverse Resort & Spa, *Grand Traverse, Michigan*

*My experience with Maple Leaf Farms is the consistent flavor and moisture of the duck. My favorite spice used with this product is cinnamon in the fall and fennel in the summer. It is an awesome product!*

Michael DeMaria — *Chef*
Michael's Catering, *Phoenix, Arizona*

*Maple Leaf duck has superior flavor, texture, and consistency to any other product I have compared it to. We have been featuring their Natural Gold Label line for over three years.*

Michael Rusconi — *Executive Chef*
Lon's at the Hermosa Inn, *Phoenix-Scottsdale, Arizona*

*Duck is one of the most favorful proteins! Cook your duck breast medium-rare and enjoy always!!*

Scott Tompkins — *Owner/Chef*
Skye Restaurant, *Peoria, Arizona*

*Maple Leaf Farms duck products bring a high quality product to every chef's door. Whether it is a half roasted duck or a flavor-infused duck breast item, they always make a memorable meal. Our guests always enjoy duck when we serve it for lunch, dinner, or a banquet, especially when it has the Maple Leaf Farms name on it.*

Michael Garbin — *CEC AAC/Executive Chef*
Union League Club of Chicago

*"Many things have changed since Maple Leaf Farms was founded fifty years ago. The technological advancements we have made in how we care for and market our ducks are tremendous," says CEO Terry Tucker. "What has not changed is our recipe for success. Throughout our fifty-year history, our company and our family have been focused on quality."*

# Chinese New Year

Hot and Sour Soup

Cucumber Salad

Szechwan Noodles and Vegetables

Spring Rolls and Pot Stickers with Chinese Barbecue Sauce

Roast Chinese Duck

Shanghai Duck Stir-Fry

Almond Cookies

*Wine:* CÔTES DU RHÔNE, SUCH AS M. CHAPOUTIER BELLERUCHE ROUGE

The flavor intensity of these Chinese classics needs a wine with similar impact, so of course reach first for the Côtes du Rhône. Made from a blend of red varieties, these wines have cherry, pepper, and smoke notes that are an essential foil for the flavors on the plate.

# Hot and Sour Soup

1 tablespoon vegetable oil

4 ounces shiitake or button
    mushrooms, stems
    discarded, caps
    thinly sliced

2 thin carrots, very thinly
    sliced on the diagonal

4 cups duck stock or
    chicken broth

3 tablespoons seasoned
    rice vinegar

2 tablespoons soy sauce

1 teaspoon hot chile oil or
    $1/2$ teaspoon crushed red
    pepper flakes

1 cup shredded cooked
    pork or duck

$1/2$ cup drained canned
    bamboo shoots, cut into
    thin strips

$1 1/2$ teaspoons dark
    sesame oil

4 ounces firm tofu, cut into
    $1/2$-inch cubes

2 tablespoons cornstarch

2 tablespoons cold water

1 egg white, beaten

2 medium green onions,
    thinly sliced on
    the diagonal

Heat oil in a large saucepan over medium heat. Add mushrooms and carrots; cook 5 minutes, stirring frequently. Add stock, vinegar, soy sauce and hot chile oil; bring to a boil over high heat. Reduce heat; simmer, uncovered, 5 minutes or until carrots are tender. Stir in pork, bamboo shoots and sesame oil; heat through. Stir in tofu. Combine cornstarch with cold water in a small bowl, mixing until smooth. Stir mixture into soup. Simmer, stirring frequently, until soup thickens slightly, about 3 minutes. Remove from heat. Stirring constantly in one direction, slowly pour egg white in a thin stream into soup. Stir in green onions; serve immediately.

Note: Seasoned rice vinegar and hot chile oil are available in the ethnic section of the supermarket.

*Makes 4 servings, about 6 cups soup*

# Cucumber Salad

1 large (12- to 14-ounce)
   seedless (hot house) cucumber

1/3 cup very thinly sliced small white onion

2 tablespoons rice vinegar

2 tablespoons vegetable oil

1 1/2 tablespoons soy sauce

1 teaspoon sugar

1 clove garlic, minced

1/4 teaspoon crushed red pepper
   flakes (optional)

Score cucumber lengthwise with tines of fork. Cut crosswise into thin slices on the diagonal; transfer to a medium bowl. Add onion to bowl. Combine vinegar, oil, soy sauce, sugar, garlic and, if desired, pepper flakes in a small bowl; mix well. Add to cucumber mixture; toss well. Cover; chill at least 4 hours or up to 24 hours before serving.

Note: Cucumber salad may be served over lettuce leaves, if desired.

*Makes 4 servings, about 3 cups*

# Szechwan Noodles and Vegetables

5 ounces (1/2 of a 10-ounce
   package) curly
   Chinese noodles

1 tablespoon vegetable oil

3 cloves garlic, minced

2 teaspoons minced fresh
   gingerroot

1/2 teaspoon crushed red
   pepper flakes (optional)

1 small red bell pepper, cut
   into thin strips

6 ounces fresh snow pea
   pods, cut lengthwise into
   thin strips

1 (7-ounce) jar baby
   corn, drained

2 tablespoons soy sauce

2 tablespoons seasoned
   rice vinegar

2 teaspoons dark
   sesame oil

1/4 cup chopped cilantro or
   thinly sliced green onions

1/4 cup roasted peanuts or
   coarsely chopped
   cashews

Cook noodles according to package directions. Meanwhile, heat oil in a large skillet over medium heat. Add garlic, ginger, and if desired, pepper flakes; cook 1 minute. Add bell pepper and pea pods; cook 5 minutes, stirring occasionally. Stir in corn, soy sauce and vinegar; heat through. Drain noodles; return to same pot. Add sesame oil; toss well. Add vegetable mixture; toss again and transfer to a large serving platter or bowl. Top with cilantro and peanuts.

Note: Chinese curly noodles and seasoned rice vinegar are available in the ethnic section of the supermarket. If the noodles are not available, substitute 5 ounces of thin spaghetti, broken in half.

*Makes 4 servings*

Chinese New Year

# Spring Rolls and Pot Stickers with Chinese Barbecue Sauce

$1/2$ cup hoisin sauce

1 medium green onion, minced

2 tablespoons seasoned rice vinegar

2 teaspoons Chinese chili sauce or chili
   garlic sauce

1 teaspoon grated fresh gingerroot

8 to 12 Maple Leaf Farms Frozen
   Spring Rolls

8 to 12 Maple Leaf Farms Frozen
   Pot Stickers

Combine hoisin sauce, green onion, vinegar, chili sauce and gingerroot in a small bowl; mix well. Prepare spring rolls and pot stickers according to package directions; serve warm with sauce for dipping.

Note: Hoisin sauce, seasoned rice vinegar and Chinese chili sauce are available in the ethnic section of the supermarket.

*Makes 4 servings*

# Roast Chinese Duck

1 (5-pound) Maple Leaf Farms Duck,
    thawed if frozen

1/3 cup orange marmalade

2 tablespoons soy sauce

2 tablespoons dry sherry or sake

1 tablespoon minced fresh gingerroot

Orange slices and chives or green onions

Remove giblets and orange sauce packet from duck; reserve for another use. Rinse duck; pat dry with paper towels. Place, breast side up, on rack of broiler pan. Roast according to package directions.

Meanwhile, combine marmalade, soy sauce, sherry and gingerroot in a bowl. Set aside half of mixture to serve with duck. Remove duck from oven; heat broiler to high. Carefully pour off drippings from bottom of broiler pan. Brush remaining marmalade mixture over duck. Broil 5 to 6 inches from heat source 5 minutes or until golden brown and bubbly. Heat reserved marmalade mixture in a saucepan over low heat until hot. Cut duck into quarters and transfer to serving plates. Serve warm marmalade mixture with duck. Garnish with orange slices and chives.

*Makes 4 servings*

*When roasting a whole duck, place it on a rack in a pan, so the fat can drain freely into the bottom of the pan and the duck doesn't sit in it.*

# Shanghai Duck Stir-Fry

4 (6-ounce) Maple Leaf
  Farms Boneless,
  Skinless Duck
  Breast Filets
4 cloves garlic, minced
2 teaspoons minced fresh
  gingerroot
5 tablespoons soy
  sauce, divided
$\frac{1}{4}$ cup duck stock or
  chicken broth
1 tablespoon cornstarch

2 tablespoons vegetable oil
1 large yellow or red bell
  pepper, cut into short,
  thin strips
2 cups fresh sugar snap
  peas or snow pea pods
1 cup cut fresh asparagus
  spears or small
  broccoli florets
4 cups hot cooked
  white rice

Cut duck crosswise into $\frac{1}{4}$-inch thick strips; place in a medium bowl. Add garlic, ginger and 2 tablespoons of the soy sauce; toss well and set aside. Combine remaining 3 tablespoons soy sauce, stock and cornstarch in a small bowl; mix until smooth and set aside.

Heat oil in a large deep skillet or wok over medium-high heat. Add bell pepper, sugar snap peas and asparagus; stir-fry 3 to 4 minutes or until vegetables are tender-crisp. Transfer to a bowl; set aside. Add duck mixture to skillet; stir-fry 4 to 5 minutes or until duck is cooked through. Return vegetables to skillet. Stir soy sauce mixture; add to skillet and stir-fry 1 to 2 minutes or until sauce thickens. Serve over rice.

Note: If desired, stir-fry mixture may be served wrapped in large Boston lettuce leaves rather than over the rice.

*Makes 4 servings*

# Almond Cookies

36 whole blanched almonds

1½ cups confectioners'
    sugar

1 cup unsalted
    butter, softened

1 teaspoon almond extract

1¾ cups all-purpose flour

2 tablespoons cornstarch

¼ teaspoon salt

1 large egg, well beaten

Fresh pineapple wedges,
    sliced ripe mango,
    clusters of red
    seedless grapes

Heat oven to 375 degrees. Arrange almonds in a single layer on a cookie sheet; bake until golden brown, about 10 minutes. Remove from oven; set aside to cool.

Beat together confectioners' sugar and butter in large bowl of electric mixer until well blended. Beat in extract. Gradually beat in combined flour, cornstarch and salt. (Mixture should hold together. If dry, beat in 1 tablespoon milk or water. If wet, beat in 1 tablespoon additional flour.)

Form levelly measured tablespoonfuls of dough into balls; place 2 inches apart on ungreased cookie sheets. Use the bottom of a glass to flatten dough to ½-inch thickness. Press an almond into the center of each cookie. Brush tops with beaten egg. Bake 12 to 14 minutes or until golden brown. Let stand on cookie sheets for 2 minutes; transfer to wire cooling racks and cool completely. Store cookies tightly covered at room temperature up to 3 days or freeze up to 3 months. Serve cookies with a platter of fresh pineapple wedges, sliced ripe mango and clusters of red seedless grapes.

*Makes 3 dozen cookies*

A duck egg is about 2 grams larger than a chicken egg. Many pastry chefs like to use duck eggs when baking because of their volume.

# Valentine's Day

French Onion Soup

Roast Asparagus with Romano Cheese

Artichokes with Mustard Aïoli

Saffron-Scented Rice

Whipped Sweet Potatoes

Garlic Mashed Potatoes

Maple-Glazed Duck Breast with Gingered Cranberry Pear Chutney

Duck with Port Stilton Cheese Sauce

Chocolate Decadence Pots de Crème

**Wine:** SPANISH RIOJA, SUCH AS MARQUES DE CACERES CRIANZA

Rioja is simply one of the best companions for duck. These recipes have some sweet, savory, and delicate elements, and rioja will complement all facets of these recipes.

# French Onion Soup

2 tablespoons duck drippings or butter

2 large Vidalia or sweet onions, thinly sliced

2 tablespoons dry sherry

2¹/₂ cups duck stock

Salt and freshly ground black
   pepper (optional)

2 slices Italian or French bread, toasted

2 slices or ¹/₂ cup shredded Jarlsberg or
   Swiss cheese

Heat drippings in a large heavy saucepan over high heat. Add onion; cover and cook until onions are wilted, about 5 minutes, stirring once. Uncover; reduce heat and continue to cook until onions are softened and golden brown, 18 to 20 minutes, stirring frequently. Add sherry; cook 3 minutes, stirring once. Add duck stock; bring to a boil over high heat. Reduce heat; simmer 20 minutes.

Heat broiler. If desired, season soup with salt and pepper to taste; ladle into two 12-ounce ovenproof serving bowls. Place one slice of toast in each bowl; top with cheese. Broil 3 to 4 inches from heat source until cheese is melted and golden brown, 3 to 4 minutes.

Note: A combination of one 10³/₄-ounce can beef consommé or 1¹/₄ cups rich beef stock and 1¹/₄ cups chicken stock or broth may be substituted for the duck stock.

*Makes 2 servings*

# Roast Asparagus with Romano Cheese

1 (8- to 10-ounce) bunch asparagus spears,
   ends trimmed

2 tablespoons butter, melted

1/4 teaspoon salt

1/4 teaspoon freshly ground black pepper

1/4 cup grated Romano cheese, preferably
   imported Pecorino Romano

Heat oven to 375 degrees. Place asparagus in a shallow baking dish or casserole. Drizzle butter and sprinkle salt and pepper over asparagus. Roast in oven until asparagus is tender-crisp, 10 to 12 minutes, depending on thickness of asparagus. Sprinkle cheese over asparagus; return to oven for 1 minute or until cheese is melted.

*Makes 2 servings*

*While duck is poultry, it is very different from chicken and turkey, because it's a red meat. This means that a well-prepared duck breast eats more like steak than chicken and is pink in the center when properly cooked to an internal temperature of 160 degrees.*

# Artichokes with Mustard Aïoli

2 artichokes, stems trimmed

1 lemon

1 tablespoon olive oil

2¹/₂ teaspoons dried tarragon, divided

3 tablespoons mayonnaise

2 tablespoons stone-ground or
   coarse-grain mustard

¹/₄ teaspoon sugar

1 small clove garlic, minced

Using kitchen shears, trim off and discard the sharp ends from artichoke leaves. Place artichokes in a large saucepan or Dutch oven. Finely shred 1 teaspoon lemon peel from lemon; place in a small bowl. Cut lemon in half; squeeze juice over artichokes in saucepan and add the lemon halves to the pan. Pour oil and sprinkle 2 teaspoons of the tarragon over artichokes. Add enough cold water to pan to cover artichokes. Cover; bring to a boil over high heat. Reduce heat; simmer, covered, until artichokes are tender, 50 to 55 minutes.

Meanwhile for aïoli, add mayonnaise, mustard, sugar, garlic and remaining ¹/₂ teaspoon tarragon to bowl with the shredded lemon peel; mix well. Drain artichokes; serve with aïoli.

*Makes 2 servings*

# Saffron-Scented Rice

$1/4$ teaspoon saffron threads

1 cup chicken or vegetable broth

2 tablespoons butter

$1/4$ cup chopped shallots or sweet onion

$1/2$ cup jasmine or long grain white rice

Salt (optional)

1 tablespoon sliced unblanched
    almonds, toasted

Crush saffron threads and stir into broth in a measuring cup; set aside. Melt butter in a medium saucepan over medium heat. Add shallots; cook 3 minutes, stirring occasionally. Stir in rice; cook 1 minute. Add saffron broth; bring to a simmer. Cover; reduce heat and simmer until liquid is absorbed, about 18 minutes. Turn off heat; let stand, covered, 5 minutes before serving. Season to taste with salt and garnish with almonds.

*Makes 2 servings*

# Whipped Sweet Potatoes

1 pound sweet potatoes, peeled and
    cut into 3/4-inch chunks
1/4 cup heavy cream or half-and-half
2 tablespoons butter
1/2 teaspoon salt
1/8 teaspoon nutmeg

Place potatoes in a medium saucepan; add enough water to pan to cover potatoes. Cover; bring to a boil over high heat. Reduce heat; simmer, covered, until potatoes are very tender, about 12 minutes.

Drain potatoes in a colander. Add cream and butter to same saucepan; place over low heat and stir mixture until butter is melted. Return potatoes to pan; add salt and nutmeg. Using a potato masher or handheld blender, mash potatoes until light and fluffy.

Note: Potatoes may be prepared up to 24 hours before serving. Cool, cover and refrigerate potatoes before reheating. Chilled potatoes may be placed in a pastry bag fitted with a large star tip, piped attractively onto a microwave-safe serving plate and heated in the microwave oven just before serving.

*Makes about 2 cups*

# Garlic Mashed Potatoes

1 pound red potatoes, peeled and
    cut into 3/4-inch chunks
3 large garlic cloves, peeled
1/4 cup heavy cream or half-and-half
2 tablespoons butter
1/2 teaspoon salt

Place potatoes and garlic cloves in a medium saucepan; add enough water to pan to cover potatoes. Cover; bring to a boil over high heat. Reduce heat; simmer, covered, until potatoes are very tender, about 18 minutes.

Drain potatoes and garlic in a colander. Add cream and butter to same saucepan; place over low heat and stir mixture until butter is melted. Return potatoes and garlic to pan; add salt. Using a potato masher or handheld blender, mash potatoes until light and fluffy.

Note: Potatoes may be prepared up to 24 hours before serving. Cool, cover and refrigerate potatoes before reheating. Chilled potatoes may be placed in a pastry bag fitted with a large star tip, piped attractively onto a microwave-safe serving plate and heated in the microwave oven just before serving.

*Makes about 2 cups*

# Maple-Glazed Duck Breast with Gingered Cranberry Pear Chutney

2 (7.5-ounce) Maple Leaf
  Farms Boneless Duck
  Breast Filets, thawed
  if frozen
1/4 teaspoon salt
1/4 teaspoon freshly ground
  black pepper

1 1/2 tablespoons pure
  maple syrup
2/3 cup Gingered Cranberry
  Pear Chutney
1 teaspoon finely shredded
  fresh gingerroot

Heat oven to 375 degrees. Score the skin of the duck breast taking care not to puncture the meat (see glossary). Heat an ovenproof skillet over medium heat until hot. Place duck in skillet skin sides down. Sprinkle salt and pepper lightly over duck. Cook 8 to 9 minutes or until skin is crispy and golden brown. Turn duck; continue cooking 3 minutes. Transfer duck to a plate; set aside. Carefully pour off drippings from skillet into a jar with a tight-fitting lid. Refrigerate duck drippings for another use. Spread syrup over seasoned meaty sides of duck and return to skillet skin side up. Transfer skillet to oven. Bake 8 to 10 minutes or until internal temperature of duck reaches 155 degrees. Transfer duck to carving board; cover with foil and let stand 5 minutes. (Internal temperature of duck will rise to 160 degrees.)

Carve duck crosswise into thin slices. Transfer to warm serving plates. Garnish with shredded gingerroot and serve with warmed or room temperature chutney.

*Makes 2 servings*

## Gingered Cranberry Pear Chutney

2 firm red or green
  Bartlett pears
1/3 cup dried cranberries
2 tablespoons brown sugar
1 tablespoon cider vinegar

2 teaspoons minced fresh
  gingerroot
1/8 teaspoon salt
1/8 teaspoon ground
  allspice

Peel, core and coarsely chop pears. Combine pears, cranberries, brown sugar, vinegar, ginger, salt and allspice in a medium saucepan. Cover; bring to a simmer over high heat. Reduce heat to low and simmer, covered, until pears are tender, about 10 minutes. Uncover; simmer over medium-high heat until chutney thickens, 3 to 4 minutes. Chutney may be prepared up to 24 hours before serving. Cool, cover and chill until serving time. Serve the chutney at room temperature or reheat the chutney just before serving.

*Makes about 1 1/4 cups chutney*

27

Valentine's Day

# Duck with
# Port Stilton Cheese Sauce

2 (12-ounce) Maple Leaf Farms Fully Cooked
Rotisserie Duck Halves, thawed if frozen

$1/2$ cup good quality port wine

3 tablespoons butter, cut into 6 pieces

$1/4$ cup plus 2 tablespoons crumbled Stilton
or Gorgonzola cheese, divided

1 tablespoon chopped fresh thyme

Heat oven to 375 degrees. Remove duck from packaging and place
in a shallow roasting pan. Bake 25 minutes or until heated through.

Meanwhile, bring wine to a boil in a medium saucepan. Boil gently
until wine is reduced to $1/4$ cup, 4 to 5 minutes. To enrich and thicken the
sauce, turn heat under saucepan to low; add 1 piece of butter at a time,
stirring until each piece melts before adding another. Remove from heat;
stir in $1/4$ cup of the cheese.

Transfer duck to two serving plates. Spoon sauce over duck and top
with remaining 2 tablespoons cheese and thyme.

*Makes 2 servings*

*The secret to having crispy duck breast skin is to score the skin (being
careful not to pierce the meat) and sauté the breast on its skin side
over low heat, so the fat has a chance to render (melt) out of the skin.
Low and slow is the way to go.*

*Rubbing the skin of a raw duck with paprika also helps to create
a golden, crispy skin when roasting.*

# Chocolate Decadence
# Pots de Crème

2 large egg yolks

3 tablespoons sugar

$1/2$ teaspoon pure vanilla extract

$1/8$ teaspoon salt

$2/3$ cup heavy whipping cream

2 ounces bittersweet chocolate candy bar,
   finely chopped

2 tablespoons sweetened whipped cream

2 teaspoons shaved bittersweet chocolate

2 strawberries, halved

Heat oven to 325 degrees. In a medium bowl, whisk together egg yolks, sugar, vanilla and salt. In a small saucepan, bring cream just to a simmer. Remove from heat; add chopped chocolate, stirring until chocolate is completely melted. Stir a small amount of egg mixture into chocolate mixture; gradually pour chocolate mixture into egg mixture in bowl, whisking constantly.

Pour mixture into two pots de crème cups or $3^1/2$-ounce ramekins about 3 inches in diameter. Place cups in a small baking pan. Pour enough hot tap water into baking pan to come halfway up sides of cups. Bake until center is barely set and jiggles slightly when shaken, 35 to 40 minutes. Remove cups from water bath; let stand at room temperature until cool. Cover; refrigerate at least 2 hours or up to 24 hours before serving. Transfer cups to small serving plates; top with whipped cream and shaved chocolate. Garnish with halved strawberries.

*Makes 2 servings*

MAPLE LEAF FARMS

# Cocktail Party

Jerk Duck Salad

Duck Bruschetta

Duck Skewers with Sweet and Spicy Dipping Sauce

Southwest Tomatillo and Duck Triangles

Chocolate Coconut Tartlets

**Wine:** CALIFORNIA CHENIN BLANC, SUCH AS DRY CREEK VINEYARDS

For a cocktail party, you want a wine that will complement the many flavors of the canapés but that has enough character to refresh your guests. Chenin blanc is a great choice.

# Jerk Duck Salad

2 teaspoons sugar

1 teaspoon dried thyme

1 teaspoon ground allspice

1/4 teaspoon salt

1/4 teaspoon
cayenne pepper

1/4 teaspoon
ground nutmeg

1/8 teaspoon ground cloves

2 (5-ounce) Maple Leaf
Farms Skinless,
Boneless Duck Breast
Filets, thawed if frozen

1 tablespoon olive oil

1/3 cup finely
chopped onion

1/2 cup chopped
cooked ham

1/2 cup chopped
fresh pineapple

1 medium tomato,
seeded, chopped

1/4 cup sour cream

30 Belgian endive leaves

In a medium bowl, combine sugar, thyme, allspice, salt, cayenne pepper, nutmeg and cloves; mix well. Cut duck into 1/4-inch cubes; add to bowl and toss with spice mixture.

Heat oil in a large skillet over medium heat. Add duck mixture and onion. Cook until duck is no longer pink and onion begins to brown, stirring frequently. Transfer to a clean bowl; cover and refrigerate until cold.

To serve, add ham, pineapple, tomato and sour cream to duck mixture; toss well. Spoon mixture onto endive leaves; arrange on a serving platter.

*Makes 30 salad-filled leaves*

# Duck Bruschetta

1/2 cup olive oil, divided

24 (1/4-inch-thick) slices French
bread baguette

1/4 cup roasted garlic purée

3/4 cup (3 ounces) feta cheese, crumbled

1 (12-ounce) jar roasted red bell peppers,
drained, cut into thin strips

4 (3-ounce) links Maple Leaf Farms Fully
Cooked Country Garlic Flavored Duck
Sausages, sliced

1 tablespoon finely chopped parsley

Heat oven to 400 degrees. Brush 1/4 cup of the oil over bread slices; arrange in a single layer on cookie or baking sheets. Spread garlic purée over slices; top with cheese, bell pepper strips and sliced duck sausage. Drizzle remaining 1/4 cup oil over bruschetta. Bake 6 to 8 minutes or until hot. Garnish with parsley.

*Makes 24 slices bruschetta*

# Duck Skewers with Sweet and Spicy Dipping Sauce

6 (5-ounce) Maple Leaf
Farms Skinless,
Boneless Duck Breast
Filets, thawed if frozen

1/2 cup apricot preserves

1/3 cup red wine

1/4 cup olive oil

2 tablespoons
balsamic vinegar

36 small bamboo skewers

Sweet and Spicy
Dipping Sauce

2 large red bell peppers

1 large green bell pepper

10 small fresh apricots,
halved, pitted or

20 chunks of
fresh pineapple

Cut duck breasts into 1-inch chunks; place in a shallow casserole dish or in a zip top plastic bag. Combine preserves, wine, oil and vinegar; mix well and pour over duck. Cover and marinate in the refrigerator at least 4 hours or overnight. Soak skewers in cold water to cover (this prevents them from burning on the grill). Prepare Sweet and Spicy Dipping Sauce. Cover and chill until serving time.

Prepare charcoal or gas grill. Drain duck; reserving marinade. Alternately thread duck, bell peppers and apricot halves onto drained skewers. Arrange skewers on grid over medium coals. Brush half of preserve mixture over skewers. Grill, covered, 5 minutes. Turn; brush remaining half of preserve mixture over skewers. Continue grilling, covered, 5 to 6 minutes or until duck is barely pink in center and peppers are tender-crisp. Serve with dipping sauce.

*Makes 3 dozen skewers*

*A quick and easy sauce for duck is equal parts of ginger ale and jam (peach, apricot, plum, or blackberry) and a dash of powdered ginger and garlic. Stir and microwave until heated.*

## Sweet and Spicy Dipping Sauce

1 large red bell pepper,
chopped

3/4 cup seasoned rice
vinegar

1/2 cup sugar

1/4 teaspoon salt

1/2 teaspoon crushed red
hot pepper flakes

1/4 teaspoon cornstarch

1 tablespoon finely
chopped cilantro

Combine all ingredients except cilantro in a medium saucepan. Bring to a boil over high heat. Reduce heat; simmer, uncovered, 6 to 8 minutes or until bell pepper is tender. Cool. Purée in a food processor or blender. Stir in cilantro; cover and chill until serving time.

*To serve a delicious duck pizza, make your favorite crust recipe and top it with plum sauce, chopped green onions, and any precooked duck meat. Top with a light sprinkle of fresh mozzarella or goat cheese. Bake until cheese starts to bubble. Enjoy!*

# Southwest Tomatillo and Duck Triangles

8 (6-inch) flour tortillas, quartered

4 cups shredded boneless Maple Leaf
   Farms Fully Cooked Rotisserie Half Duck
   or Duck Leg Confit

1 cup chopped fresh tomatillos

1 cup chopped plum tomatoes

3 to 4 jalapeño chile peppers,
   seeded, minced

1/4 cup finely chopped cilantro

2 tablespoons fresh lime juice

2 cloves garlic, minced

1 teaspoon ground cumin

1/2 teaspoon salt

4 cups (1 pound) shredded Cheddar cheese

1 small red onion, sliced, slices quartered
   forming strips

Heat oven to 375 degrees. Arrange tortilla quarters in a single layer on cookie or baking sheets. Bake 5 to 7 minutes or until lightly toasted. Remove from oven and set aside.

Meanwhile, in a bowl combine duck, tomatillos, tomatoes, chile peppers, cilantro, lime juice, garlic, cumin and salt; mix well. Add cheese; mix well. Spoon mixture over baked tortillas; top with onion strips. Return to oven and bake 10 to 12 minutes or until cheese is melted.

*Makes 32 triangles*

# Chocolate Coconut Tartlets

1 (13-ounce) package
   coconut macaroon
   cookies (about
   18 cookies)
1 cup finely
   chopped pecans
1/3 cup butter, melted
1 (14-ounce) can
   sweetened
   condensed milk
2 tablespoons
   hazelnut liqueur

2 tablespoons water
1 (4-ounce) package
   instant chocolate pudding
   and pie filling mix
2 tablespoons unsweetened
   cocoa powder
2/3 cup heavy
   whipping cream
Whipped cream for garnish
1/4 cup sweetened
   shredded coconut,
   lightly toasted

Heat oven to 375 degrees. Grease 36 mini (1³/4-inch) muffin cups. Crumble macaroons into a medium bowl. Add pecans and melted butter; mix well. Press 1 tablespoon of the mixture into bottom and up sides of muffin cups. Bake 8 to 10 minutes or until set. Transfer to a wire cooling rack; cool completely. Run a knife around edges of crust to loosen.

In bowl of electric mixer, combine sweetened condensed milk, liqueur and water; blend on low speed. Add pudding mix and cocoa; beat at medium speed 2 minutes or until smooth. Cover; chill for 5 minutes.

In a clean bowl of electric mixer, beat ²/3 cup whipping cream to soft peaks. Fold in chocolate mixture. Mound into crusts. Cover and chill at least 2 hours or overnight. Just before serving, garnish with additional whipped cream and toasted coconut.

*Makes 3 dozen tartlets*

MAPLE LEAF FARMS

# Family Reunion

Mesclun Salad with Basil Parmesan Vinaigrette

Grilled Vegetable Skewers

Roasted Vegetable Medley

Spicy Garlic Duck Breast

Duck and Vegetable Lasagna

Cherry Crisp

Old-Fashioned Carrot Cake

---

**Wine:** ITALIAN SANGIOVESE, SUCH AS UMBERTO CESARI, EMILIA ROMAGNA

Sangiovese is a fantastic food wine and a natural with these recipes. The lively acidity, abundant fruit, and natural earthiness of this wine really work well with the pasta, vegetables, and, of course, the duck.

## Mesclun Salad with Basil Parmesan Vinaigrette

1 cup extra virgin olive oil

$^1/_3$ cup balsamic vinegar

1 teaspoon finely grated orange peel

2 cloves garlic, minced

$1^1/_4$ teaspoons salt

$^1/_2$ teaspoon freshly ground black pepper

$^1/_4$ cup grated Parmesan cheese

$^1/_4$ cup minced fresh basil leaves

1 pound mesclun salad greens or mixed
  salad greens (24 cups packed)

Whisk together oil, vinegar, orange peel, garlic, salt and pepper in a bowl until well combined. (At this point dressing may be covered and refrigerated up to 2 days.) Just before serving, stir Parmesan cheese and basil into dressing. Toss with mesclun.

*Makes 12 servings*

## Grilled Vegetable Skewers

2 pounds small red potatoes or halved
  medium-sized potatoes

1 pound baby green pattypan squash

1 pound baby yellow pattypan squash

2 large red bell peppers, cut into
  1-inch chunks

$^1/_2$ cup olive oil

4 cloves garlic, minced

2 teaspoons salt

1 teaspoon freshly ground black pepper

$^1/_2$ cup chopped fresh basil or chives or
  a combination

Prepare charcoal or gas grill. Cook the potatoes in a large pot of simmering salted water for 6 minutes. Add squash; continue cooking for 2 minutes or until vegetables are tender-crisp. Drain and rinse with cold water to stop the cooking.

Alternately thread the potatoes, squash and bell pepper chunks onto metal skewers. Combine oil, garlic, salt and pepper in a small bowl; mix well. Brush mixture over both sides of vegetables. Grill on a covered grill for 5 minutes per side or until vegetables are tender. Top with basil.

Note: Zucchini and/or yellow summer squash may be substituted. Cut squash into $^3/_4$-inch-thick slices. Reduce simmering time to 1 minute.

*Makes 12 servings*

# Roasted Vegetable Medley

3 pounds red potatoes, cut into
   1-inch chunks

1/4 cup rendered duck fat or olive oil

2 medium onions, cut through stems into
   1/2-inch-thick wedges

1 pound baby carrots

4 cloves garlic, minced

1 teaspoon salt

1/2 teaspoon freshly ground black pepper

1/4 cup chopped chives or parsley (optional)

Heat oven to 400 degrees. Toss potatoes with duck fat or oil in a bowl and arrange in a single layer in two shallow roasting pans (one pan may be the bottom of a broiler pan). Transfer to oven and roast 20 minutes.

Add onions, carrots, garlic, salt and pepper to potatoes; toss well. Return to oven and continue roasting 20 to 25 minutes or until vegetables are tender. Top with chives or parsley, if desired.

*Makes 12 servings*

*Most Maple Leaf Farms ducks are raised on small family farms, many of which are Amish or Mennonite, by growers who have been trained and certified concerning duck care and behavior.*

*Summer version (grilled): Prepare charcoal or gas grill. Place partially cooked duck skin sides down on grid over medium coals. Grill on a covered grill 5 minutes. Turn duck; continue to grill, covered, until internal temperature of duck registers 160 degrees. Transfer duck to serving plates.*

*Fall version (roasted): Heat oven to 375 degrees. Place partially cooked duck skin sides up in a jelly roll pan or roasting pan. Bake 12 to 14 minutes or until internal temperature of duck reaches 160 degrees. Transfer duck to serving plates.*

# Spicy Garlic Duck Breast

2 teaspoons dried thyme leaves

3/4 teaspoon salt

3/4 teaspoon freshly ground black pepper

3/4 teaspoon cayenne pepper

12 (7.5-ounce) Maple Leaf Farms Roasted
Garlic Marinated Boneless Duck Breast
Filets, thawed if frozen

Combine thyme leaves, salt, pepper and cayenne pepper in a small bowl; set aside. Drain duck; pat dry with paper towels. Score the skin of the duck breasts, taking care not to puncture the meat (see glossary).

Heat a large skillet over medium heat until hot. Place 4 duck breast filets in skillet skin sides down. Sprinkle 1/3 of the spice mixture over meaty sides of duck. Cook 8 minutes or until skin is crisp and golden brown. Turn duck; continue cooking 3 minutes. Transfer duck to a plate; carefully pour off drippings from skillet into a jar with a tight-fitting lid. Repeat twice with remaining duck and spice mixture. Refrigerate the spicy flavored drippings for another use. (At this point, duck may be covered and refrigerated up to 8 hours before grilling or roasting. Let stand at room temperature 30 minutes.)

*Makes 12 servings*

# Duck and Vegetable Lasagna

8 (12-ounce) Maple Leaf
    Farms Duck Leg
    Quarters, thawed
    if frozen
1 pound asparagus
    spears, cut into
    $3/4$-inch pieces
2 large yellow bell
    peppers, cut into
    $3/4$-inch pieces
2 (26-ounce) jars tomato
    basil or marinara
    pasta sauce

$1/4$ cup butter
$1/4$ cup all-purpose flour
4 cups (1 quart) heavy
    whipping cream
$1/2$ teaspoon salt
12 long curly lasagna
    noodles, cooked
    according to package
    directions
$1 1/2$ cups freshly grated
    Parmesan cheese
$1/2$ cup chopped
    fresh basil

Heat oven to 350 degrees. Place duck in a shallow roasting pan large enough to hold the duck in a single layer. Cover pan with heavy aluminum foil. Place in oven; bake $1 1/2$ hours. Uncover pan; sprinkle asparagus and bell peppers over duck. Cover with foil; continue to bake 15 minutes or until vegetables are tender and internal temperature of duck reaches 180 degrees. Uncover; cool mixture in pan.

When cool enough to handle, remove duck from pan. Using a slotted spoon, transfer vegetables from roasting pan to a large bowl. Discard skin and bones from duck and shred or cut meat into chunks. Add pasta sauce and duck to vegetables in bowl. (Sauce may be refrigerated up to 24 hours before assembling lasagna. Let stand at room temperature 30 minutes.)

To prepare the béchamel sauce, melt butter in a medium saucepan over medium heat. Add flour; cook and stir 1 minute. Add cream and salt; bring to a simmer, stirring frequently. Simmer 5 minutes or until sauce thickens, stirring frequently. Remove from heat; let stand 10 minutes.

Spoon 1 cup of the duck sauce over bottom of each of two 13x9-inch glass baking dishes or 3-quart casserole dishes. In each dish, layer 3 noodles, a scant $1/2$ cup of the béchamel sauce, $1/4$ cup of the Parmesan cheese and 2 cups duck sauce. Repeat layering once. Sprinkle remaining $1/4$ cup Parmesan cheese over each dish.

Bake lasagna, covered loosely with foil, in a 350-degree oven for 45 to 50 minutes or until hot and bubbly. Let stand 5 minutes before serving. Top with basil.

*Makes 12 servings*

# Cherry Crisp

1$^{1}/_{2}$ cups granulated sugar

3 tablespoons cornstarch

4 (14$^{1}/_{2}$-ounce) cans drained pitted sour
cherries or 2$^{1}/_{2}$ pounds frozen pitted sour
cherries, thawed, drained

$^{1}/_{2}$ teaspoon almond extract

1$^{1}/_{4}$ cups all-purpose flour

1 cup packed light brown sugar

1 cup old-fashioned or quick oats, uncooked

$^{3}/_{4}$ cup unsalted butter, cut into pieces

$^{1}/_{2}$ teaspoon salt

$^{1}/_{2}$ cup sliced almonds

Vanilla or cinnamon ice cream (optional)

Heat oven to 375 degrees. In a large bowl, combine granulated sugar and cornstarch, mixing well. Add cherries and extract; mix well. Pour mixture into a 13×9-inch glass baking dish or 3-quart casserole dish.

In bowl of food processor, combine flour, brown sugar, oats, butter and salt. Process just until mixture is finely crumbled. Sprinkle mixture evenly over cherry mixture; top with almonds. Bake 50 to 60 minutes or until topping is golden brown and cherry mixture is bubbly. Let stand at least 30 minutes before serving. Serve warm or at room temperature with ice cream, if desired.

Note: If food processor is not available, combine ingredients in a large bowl and cut in butter with a pastry blender or two knives until coarse crumbs appear.

*Makes 12 servings*

"Bombay Duck" is not a duck at all! It is actually dried salted fish found in East Indian and some specialty markets.

# Old-Fashioned Carrot Cake

**CAKE**

2 cups all-purpose flour

2 teaspoons baking powder

1 1/2 teaspoons cinnamon

1 teaspoon baking soda

1/2 teaspoon salt

1/2 teaspoon ground cloves

1/2 teaspoon ground allspice

1/2 teaspoon ground nutmeg

1/2 teaspoon ground ginger

1 1/4 cups canola or
vegetable oil

1 1/2 cups granulated sugar

4 large eggs

2 cups finely grated carrots
(about 3 large carrots)

1 (8-ounce) can chopped
pineapple, drained

1 cup chopped walnuts

**ICING**

1 cup confectioners' sugar

4 ounces cream
cheese, softened

1 teaspoon pure
vanilla extract

1/3 cup (or more) heavy
whipping cream

1/3 cup chopped
walnuts, toasted

For cake, preheat oven to 350 degrees. In a medium bowl, combine flour, baking powder, cinnamon, baking soda, salt, cloves, allspice, nutmeg and ginger. Stir well and set aside.

In large bowl of electric mixer combine oil and granulated sugar; beat at medium speed until well blended. Beat in eggs one at a time. Beat in carrots and pineapple. On low speed, gradually blend in flour mixture, then walnuts (batter will be thick).

Transfer batter to a greased and floured 12-cup bundt pan. Bake 45 minutes or until wooden pick inserted in center comes out clean. Transfer to a wire cooling rack; let stand 1 hour. Invert cake onto a serving plate; cool completely.

For icing, mix confectioners' sugar, cream cheese and vanilla until well combined. With mixer running, slowly pour in cream. Icing should be thick but pourable. If necessary, add 1 tablespoon additional cream. Spoon icing over top of cake letting excess drip attractively down sides of cake. Sprinkle toasted walnuts over top of cake. (Cake is best served the same day it is baked. Refrigerate any leftovers.)

*Makes 12 servings*

43

MAPLE LEAF FARMS

# Mexican Birthday

Tequila Sunrise Punch

Grits and Green Chile Casserole

Mexican-Style Black Beans

Duck Chipotle-Stuffed Poblano Chiles

Duck Fajitas

Mexican Birthday Cookies

*Wine:* ALSACE GEWÜRZTRAMINER, SUCH AS TRIMBACH RESERVE

The spicy, bold flavors of these recipes call for an equally intrepid wine. Gewürztraminer can handle the heat of the chiles and complement the earthier elements of the recipes as well.

# Tequila Sunrise Punch

3 cups orange juice

3 cups pineapple juice

1 1/2 cups tequila

1/4 cup fresh lime juice

Grenadine syrup

Lime slices

Maraschino cherries

In a large pitcher, combine orange juice, pineapple juice, tequila and lime juice. Chill at least 1 hour or up to 24 hours. To serve, stir mixture well and pour into tall glasses over ice. Drizzle about 1 tablespoon grenadine syrup over each serving. Garnish with lime slices and cherries as desired.

Note: For a nonalcoholic version, substitute 3/4 cup additional orange juice and 3/4 cup pineapple juice for the tequila.

*Makes 6 to 8 servings*

*Did you know that Duck Sauce is actually plum sauce? It's usually made with plums, apricots, sugar, and seasonings.*

# Grits and Green Chile Casserole

2¹/₂ cups duck or chicken stock or broth

1¹/₂ cups quick-cooking grits

1 cup sour cream

2 (4-ounce) cans chopped green
   chiles, undrained

Salt (optional)

1¹/₂ cups shredded Monterey Jack
   cheese, divided

Chopped cilantro (optional)

Heat oven to 375 degrees. Bring stock or broth to a boil in a heavy medium saucepan over high heat. Gradually stir in grits. Reduce heat to low; cook 6 minutes or until very thick, stirring frequently. Remove from heat; stir in sour cream and chiles. Season with salt if desired.

Spread half of grits into a round 1¹/₂-quart casserole or soufflé dish. Sprinkle 1 cup of the cheese over grits; repeat layering with remaining grits and ¹/₂ cup cheese. Bake 30 minutes or until cheese is melted and beginning to brown. Garnish with cilantro, if desired. Cut into 6 wedges to serve.

*Makes 6 servings*

# Mexican-Style Black Beans

1 tablespoon vegetable oil

1 medium onion, chopped

1 large red bell pepper, chopped

4 cloves garlic, minced

2 (16-ounce) cans black beans, drained

3/4 cup bottled salsa

1/2 cup duck or chicken broth or water

1 teaspoon ground cumin

Chopped cilantro (optional)

Heat oil in a large saucepan over medium heat. Add onion; cook 5 minutes, stirring occasionally. Add bell pepper and garlic; cook 5 minutes, stirring occasionally. Add beans, salsa, broth and cumin; simmer 10 minutes. (At this point beans may stand at room temperature up to 1 hour or may be refrigerated up to 24 hours before reheating.) Transfer to a serving dish; top with cilantro, if desired.

*Makes 6 servings, about 41/2 cups*

# Duck Chipotle-Stuffed Poblano Chiles

6 (12-ounce) Maple Leaf Farms Duck
    Leg Quarters, thawed if frozen
12 large fresh poblano chile peppers
2 ears fresh corn, husked
2 cups crumbled Chihuahua, queso anejo or
    shredded Monterey Jack cheese
1 cup sliced green onions
3 tablespoons puréed canned chipotle
    chiles in adobo sauce
1$^1/_2$ cups bottled salsa

Heat oven to 350 degrees. Place duck in a shallow roasting pan large enough to hold the duck in a single layer. Cover pan with heavy aluminum foil. Place in oven and bake 1$^1/_2$ to 1$^3/_4$ hours or until internal temperature of duck reaches 180 degrees. Uncover; cool. When cool enough to handle, discard bones and skin and cut or tear duck meat into $^3/_4$-inch chunks. (At this point duck may be covered and chilled up to 24 hours before assembling chiles. Let stand at room temperature 30 minutes.)

Preheat broiler. Place whole chile peppers and husked corn on a jelly roll pan or large baking sheet lined with aluminum foil. Broil 3 to 4 inches from heat source 15 to 20 minutes or until skin of peppers is evenly blackened (charred) and corn is beginning to brown, turning occasionally. Transfer corn to a cutting board. Wrap peppers in the foil from the baking pan; let stand 10 minutes to steam. When cool enough to handle, cut kernels from cob; transfer to a large bowl. Add duck, cheese, green onions and chipotle chile purée to bowl; mix well.

Peel off and discard blackened skin from peppers. Cut a lengthwise slit down one side of each pepper (do not cut peppers in half). Carefully open each pepper and pull out and discard seeds and membrane. Stuff whole peeled peppers with duck mixture; transfer to two large shallow baking dishes. Cover dishes with foil. (At this point peppers may be covered and chilled up to 8 hours before baking. Add 5 minutes to baking time if peppers are cold.) Bake in preheated 375-degree oven 25 minutes or until hot. Serve with salsa.

Note: Look for cans of chipotle chiles in adobo sauce in the ethnic section of the supermarket. Purée contents of can in a blender or food processor and store extra purée tightly covered in the refrigerator up to 1 month or freeze up to 6 months.

*Makes 6 servings, two stuffed peppers each*

*White Pekin duck is low in saturated fat. It provides 0.5 gram of saturated fat, as opposed to chicken, which has 1.0 gram of saturated fat.*

# Duck Fajitas

4 (6-ounce) Maple Leaf Farms Boneless,
    Skinless Duck Breast Filets

3 large cloves garlic, minced

2 teaspoons ground cumin

2 teaspoons chili powder

1 teaspoon salt

1/4 teaspoon cayenne pepper

2 tablespoons vegetable oil, divided

1 each red, yellow and green bell pepper,
    cut into long strips

1 medium red onion, thinly sliced

12 (6-inch) flour tortillas, warmed according
    to package directions

Optional toppings: salsa, sour cream,
    diced ripe avocado, chopped cilantro

Cut duck crosswise into 1/2-inch-thick strips; place in a medium bowl. Add garlic, cumin, chili powder, salt and cayenne pepper; mix well.

Heat 1 tablespoon of the oil in a 12-inch skillet over medium-high heat until hot. Add duck strips; stir-fry until barely pink in center, 6 to 8 minutes. Transfer to a clean bowl; set aside.

Heat remaining oil in same skillet; add bell peppers and red onion; stir-fry until tender, about 5 minutes. Return duck with any accumulated juices to skillet; stir-fry 2 minutes. Serve in tortillas with toppings as desired.

*Makes 6 servings*

# Mexican Birthday Cookies

1 cup unsalted butter

2 cups confectioners' sugar, divided

1 teaspoon pure vanilla extract

$1/2$ teaspoon salt

$1/2$ teaspoon cinnamon

2 cups all-purpose flour

1 cup ground almonds

In large bowl of electric mixer, beat butter at medium-low speed until creamy. Add $1/2$ cup of the confectioners' sugar, vanilla, salt and cinnamon; beat until well combined. Gradually beat in flour, then almonds, mixing well.

Preheat oven to 350 degrees. With hands, roll levelly measured tablespoonfuls of dough into 2-inch ropes and bend ends down to form crescent shapes. Place 1 inch apart on ungreased cookie sheets. Bake one sheet at a time 12 to 13 minutes or just until set and beginning to brown slightly. Let stand on cookie sheet 2 minutes. Transfer to wire cooling racks set over sheets of waxed paper.

Place remaining $11/2$ cups confectioners' sugar in a strainer. Shake confectioners' sugar over warm cookies to coat; cool cookies completely. Dust with additional confectioners' sugar when cooled.

Chocolate Variation: Do not coat cookies with confectioners' sugar. Cool cookies completely. Melt 8 ounces chopped semisweet or bittersweet chocolate (or chips) over low heat in a saucepan or at 50% power in bowl in a microwave oven. Dip half of each crescent in chocolate, scrape excess chocolate off bottom of cookie; place on a sheet of waxed paper and let stand or chill until chocolate is set.

*Makes about 3 dozen cookies*

MAPLE LEAF FARMS

# Garden Party

White Sangria

Crudités with Herbed Cheese Dip

Heirloom Tomato Salad

Grilled Rosemary Duck Breast Sandwiches with Onion Marmalade

Duck Tabbouleh Salad

Summer Berries Romanoff

*Wine:* BEAUJOLAIS, SUCH AS LOUIS JADOT BEAUJOLAIS VILLAGES

When served slightly chilled, beaujolais is quite versatile. The fresh, garden flavors are enhanced by the fresh, bright plum and cherry flavors of beaujolais.

# White Sangria

1 (750- milliliter) bottle dry white wine
  such as pinot grigio

$1/2$ cup Cointreau or Triple Sec

$1/2$ cup Cognac or brandy

2 small oranges, thinly sliced

2 small lemons, thinly sliced

Combine all ingredients in a large pitcher. Chill at least 2 hours or up to 24 hours before serving. Serve over ice in tall glasses, adding some of the fruit to each glass.

Variation: For Sangria Spritzers, add a splash of club soda to each glass of sangria.

*Makes 6 to 8 servings*

*Canard is the French word for "duck." In any language, Maple Leaf Farms duck means succulent quality!*

# Crudités with Herbed Cheese Dip

2 (8-ounce) packages
   cream cheese, softened
2 tablespoons prepared
   horseradish
2 tablespoons milk
1/4 cup minced mixed fresh
   herbs such as thyme,
   dill, rosemary, basil
   and parsley
3 tablespoons minced
   fresh chives or green
   onion tops
1/4 teaspoon salt

8 ounces fresh
   asparagus spears
8 ounces baby zucchini or
   pattypan squash
1 bunch radishes with
   greens attached
1 large red bell pepper
1 large yellow or orange
   bell pepper
1 bunch baby carrots
   with tops
Flowering kale or outer
   cabbage leaves
Breadsticks

Combine cream cheese, horseradish and milk in a bowl, mixing well. Add herbs, chives and salt; mix well. Transfer to a serving dish (or hollowed out red bell pepper). Dip may be covered and chilled up to 1 day before serving. Let come to room temperature before serving.

Cook asparagus in boiling water 2 minutes; add squash and continue to cook 1 to 2 minutes or until vegetables are tender-crisp. Drain and rinse in cold water. Scrub radishes, leaving greens attached. Cut bell peppers lengthwise into 1-inch-thick slices. Cut slices in half diagonally leaving curved ends intact for "scoops." Scrub carrots and trim greens leaving 1 inch of stems attached.

Line a large shallow basket or serving tray with kale or cabbage leaves. Place dip in center; surround with vegetables and breadsticks.

*Makes 6 servings*

55

# Heirloom Tomato Salad

1/4 cup extra virgin olive oil

2 tablespoons sherry vinegar or white
balsamic vinegar

1 clove garlic, minced

1/4 teaspoon salt

1/4 teaspoon freshly ground black pepper

6 large leaves red lettuce or outer leaves of
romaine lettuce

2 large yellow tomatoes

2 large red heirloom or beefsteak tomatoes

2 cups yellow or red teardrop or
cherry tomatoes

3 tablespoons chopped fresh basil

3 tablespoons pine nuts, toasted

In a small bowl, combine oil, vinegar, garlic, salt and pepper; mix well.
Cover; refrigerate at least 1 hour or up to 24 hours before serving.

Line 6 serving plates with lettuce leaves. Cut large tomatoes crosswise
into 1/4-inch-thick slices. Arrange slices attractively over lettuce leaves.
Scatter teardrop tomatoes over sliced tomatoes. Drizzle dressing evenly
over tomatoes; top with basil and pine nuts.

*Makes 6 servings*

# Grilled Rosemary Duck Breast Sandwiches with Onion Marmalade

¼ cup Dijon mustard

1 tablespoon dried
   rosemary leaves, crushed

3 cloves garlic, minced

6 (5-ounce) Maple Leaf
   Farms Skinless,
   Boneless Duck Breast
   Filets, thawed if frozen

2 tablespoons duck
   drippings or butter

2 large yellow onions,
   thinly sliced

1 tablespoon
   Worcestershire sauce

1 tablespoon light
   brown sugar

¼ teaspoon salt

¼ teaspoon freshly ground
   black pepper

6 large leaves red lettuce
   or romaine lettuce

6 individual focaccia or
   ciabatta rolls, about
   5 inches in diameter, split

Combine mustard, rosemary and garlic in a small bowl; mix well. Spread mixture evenly over both sides of duck breasts. Cover; refrigerate while preparing onion marmalade.

Heat drippings in a large nonstick skillet over medium heat. Add sliced onions; cover and cook 15 minutes or until onions are softened, stirring each 5 minutes. Stir in Worcestershire sauce, brown sugar, salt and pepper. Cook, uncovered, 5 minutes or until onions are very tender and liquid evaporates, stirring frequently. (Onions may be prepared and refrigerated up to 24 hours before serving. Let stand at room temperature 20 minutes.)

Prepare charcoal or gas grill. Arrange duck breasts on grid over medium-high coals. Grill, covered, 5 minutes. Turn; continue grilling, covered, 5 to 7 minutes or until internal temperature of duck registers 160 degrees. Transfer duck to carving board; tent with foil and let stand 5 minutes. (Internal temperature of duck will rise to 165 degrees.) Carve duck crosswise into thin slices. Place lettuce leaves on bottoms of rolls; top with sliced duck, onion marmalade and tops of rolls.

Note: If individual sizes are not available, purchase a large rectangular loaf of focaccia or ciabatta and cut into 6 rectangles before splitting in half. Rosemary or olive-flavored bread will make these sandwiches even more flavorful.

*Makes 6 servings*

# Duck Tabbouleh Salad

*White Pekin duck is lower in calories than many cuts of beef and comparable in calories to chicken and turkey.*

1¹/₂ cups uncooked bulgur wheat

3 cups boiling water

1 cup finely chopped parsley

¹/₃ cup finely chopped mint leaves

¹/₃ cup finely chopped green onions

¹/₃ cup extra virgin olive oil

3 tablespoons lemon juice

³/₄ teaspoon salt

¹/₂ teaspoon freshly ground black pepper

1 large cucumber, not peeled, seeded and finely diced

1 large tomato, seeded, finely diced

3 cups shredded boneless Maple Leaf Farms Fully Cooked Rotisserie Half Duck or Duck Leg Confit, divided

6 large leaves Boston or red leaf lettuce

6 lemon wedges

Place bulgur in a large bowl. Pour boiling water over bulgur; mix well and let stand at room temperature 30 minutes. Drain well and return bulgur to same bowl. Add parsley, mint, green onions, oil, lemon juice, salt and pepper; mix well. At this point, salad may be covered and chilled up to 24 hours before serving. Let stand at room temperature 20 minutes and proceed as recipe directs.

Stir cucumber, tomato and 2 cups of the duck meat into salad; mix well. Transfer to lettuce-lined serving plates; top with remaining duck meat. Serve with lemon wedges.

*Makes 6 servings*

# Summer Berries Romanoff

6 to 7 cups mixed berries such as
    blueberries, raspberries, sliced
    strawberries and/or blackberries

1/4 cup almond liqueur (amaretto)

1 (15- to 16-ounce) container mascarpone
    cheese, at room temperature

2 tablespoons honey

1 tablespoon confectioners' sugar

Chopped or crushed amaretti
    cookies (optional)

Fresh mint sprigs or chopped fresh mint
    leaves (optional)

In a medium bowl, combine berries with almond liqueur; mix well. Cover; chill at least 1 hour or up to 8 hours before serving.

With a handheld electric mixer or wire whisk, combine mascarpone cheese and honey in a bowl, mixing until light and fluffy. Spread mixture over bottom of 6 small serving bowls; chill at least 1 hour or up to 8 hours before serving.

About 20 minutes before serving, remove bowls of cheese from refrigerator; let stand to soften cheese. Spoon berry mixture over cheese in bowls. Place confectioners' sugar in a strainer; shake over berries. Top with cookies and garnish with mint sprigs or chopped mint, if desired.

Note: If mascarpone cheese is not available, substitute two 8-ounce packages cream cheese.

*Makes 6 servings*

MAPLE LEAF FARMS

# Fourth of July

Grilled Pepper Salad

Summer Corn with Honey Mustard Butter

Barbecued Bean Casserole

Grilled Duck with Chipotle Barbecue Sauce

Grilled Peppered Duck Breast with Citrus Mustard Sauce

All-American Apple Dumplings

*Wine:* CALIFORNIA DRY ROSÉ, SUCH AS BONNY DOON VIN GRIS

The recipes here call for a wine with plenty of red berry flavors, but the last thing you want on an 80-plus degree day is a glass of warm red wine.  What to do?  Try a fruit-packed, but dry, rosé. It's the perfect warm weather wine; just ask the French, Italians, and Spanish.

# Grilled Pepper Salad

3 medium red bell peppers

3 medium yellow or orange bell peppers

1/2 cup olive oil

1/4 cup balsamic vinegar

2 cloves garlic, minced

1/2 teaspoon salt

1/2 teaspoon sugar

1/4 teaspoon freshly ground black pepper

8 large red lettuce leaves

1/4 cup julienned or chopped fresh basil

Prepare charcoal or gas grill, or preheat broiler. Cut peppers lengthwise into quarters; discard stems and seeds. Place skin sides down on grid or skin sides up on a baking sheet. Grill over hot coals or broil 3 inches from heat source until skins are evenly blackened, about 10 minutes. Transfer peppers to a bowl; cover and let stand 10 minutes. Working over the bowl to catch any pepper juices, peel off and discard charred skins from peppers. Cut peppers into long, thick strips. Place peppers and any accumulated juices in a shallow dish.

Combine oil, vinegar, garlic, salt, sugar and pepper in a bowl; mix well. Pour over peppers. Cover; let stand at room temperature 30 minutes or refrigerate up to 1 day before serving.

Serve peppers and marinade over lettuce leaves; top with basil.

*Makes 8 servings*

# Summer Corn with Honey Mustard Butter

$1/2$ cup unsalted butter, softened

2 tablespoons Dijon mustard

1 tablespoon honey

$1/4$ teaspoon salt

$1/8$ teaspoon freshly ground black pepper

8 ears fresh corn in husks

Combine butter, mustard, honey, salt and pepper in a bowl; mix well. Transfer to a small bowl or decorative crock; cover and refrigerate until serving time. (Butter may be prepared up to 2 days before serving.)

Carefully peel back husks from corn, leaving them attached to corn. Remove and discard corn silk. Bring husks back up over each ear of corn. Soak corn in cold water to cover for 20 to 30 minutes. (This will prevent burning on grill.)

Prepare charcoal or gas grill. Drain corn. Place on grid over medium-hot coals. Grill on a covered grill 10 minutes. Turn corn with tongs; continue grilling, covered, until corn is tender and hot, 10 to 12 minutes longer. Serve corn with honey mustard butter for spreading.

*Makes 8 servings*

# Barbecued Bean Casserole

3 thick slices bacon, diced

1 medium onion, chopped

2 cups diced yellow, green or red bell
    peppers or a combination

1 (18-ounce) jar or (16-ounce) can
    baked beans

1 (15-ounce) can red or kidney
    beans, drained

1 (15-ounce) can butter beans, drained

1/3 cup packed light brown sugar

1/3 cup chili sauce or ketchup

1 tablespoon Dijon or spicy brown mustard

Cook bacon in a large deep skillet over medium heat until crisp. Use a slotted spoon to transfer about 1/4 cup of the bacon to a paper towel; reserve for garnish.

Add onion to remaining bacon and drippings in skillet. Cook 5 minutes, stirring occasionally. Add bell peppers; cook 4 minutes, stirring once. Add remaining ingredients; mix well and bring to a boil. Cover; reduce heat to low and simmer 15 minutes. Transfer to a serving dish and top with reserved bacon.

*Makes 8 servings*

# Grilled Duck with Chipotle Barbecue Sauce

4 Maple Leaf Farms Roast Half Duck,
  thawed if frozen
1/2 cup packed light brown sugar
1/2 cup chili sauce or ketchup
1 1/2 tablespoons Worcestershire sauce
1 1/2 tablespoons soy sauce
2 teaspoons puréed canned chipotle chiles
  in adobo sauce or chipotle chile powder

Unwrap duck and reserve orange sauce for another use. Combine brown sugar, chili sauce, Worcestershire sauce, soy sauce and puréed chiles in a bowl; mix well. Reserve half of sauce for serving.

Prepare charcoal or gas grill. Place duck skin sides down on grid over medium coals. Grill, covered, 10 minutes. Turn; brush remaining barbecue sauce over duck. Continue grilling, covered, 5 to 10 minutes or until duck is well browned. Cut each duck half into two servings. Serve with reserved barbecue sauce.

*Makes 8 servings*

*For wonderful barbecued flavor, try grilling outdoors. For a whole raw duck, the best results come from first precooking it in your oven (following the package directions), and for the last twenty to thirty minutes finishing it on the grill. This gives the duck a wonderfully crispy skin.*

Meals to Remember

*Did you know that the classic French orange sauce for duck is called bigarade sauce? It is a brown sauce flavored with oranges. Bigarade is French for "bitter orange," so be careful not to use overly sweet citrus in the sauce.*

# Grilled Peppered Duck Breast with Citrus Mustard Sauce

8 (7.5-ounce) Maple Leaf Farms Peppercorn
    Marinated Boneless Duck Breast Filets,
    thawed if frozen
1 teaspoon salt
1/2 cup orange marmalade
1/4 cup Dijon mustard
2 tablespoons orange juice

Score the skin of the duck breast taking care not to puncture the meat (see glossary). Heat an ovenproof skillet over medium heat until hot. Place duck in skillet, skin sides down. Sprinkle salt over duck. Cook 8 minutes or until skin is crisp and golden brown. Turn duck; continue cooking 3 minutes. Transfer duck to a plate; reserve drippings from skillet for another use. (At this point, duck may be covered and refrigerated up to 8 hours before grilling.)

Prepare charcoal or gas grill. Combine marmalade, mustard and orange juice in a bowl; mix well. Place partially cooked duck skin sides down on grid over medium coals. Grill on a covered grill 5 minutes. Turn duck; brush citrus mustard sauce over skin sides of duck. Continue to grill, covered, until internal temperature of duck registers 160 degrees. Transfer duck to serving plates; serve with reserved citrus mustard sauce.

*Makes 8 servings*

# All-American Apple Dumplings

2¼ cups all-purpose flour

3 tablespoons confectioners' sugar

½ teaspoon salt

1 cup unsalted butter, cut into pieces

8 ounces cream cheese, cubed

5 tablespoons cream or milk, divided

8 small golden delicious apples
   (5 to 6 ounces each)

⅓ cup packed brown sugar

1 teaspoon apple pie spice or cinnamon

2 tablespoons unsalted butter, melted

¼ cup finely chopped pecans

2 large egg yolks

Vanilla ice cream

Caramel or butterscotch ice cream topping

Combine flour, confectioners' sugar and salt in a food processor or large bowl. Add the butter pieces; process with on/off pulses or cut butter into dry ingredients with a pastry blender until butter is the size of small peas. Add cream cheese; continue processing or cutting in cream cheese until coarse crumbs appear. Add 3 tablespoons of the cream; process or mix just until dough comes together in a ball. Divide dough in half. Wrap each half of dough in plastic wrap; form into a round disc and refrigerate at least 30 minutes or up to 24 hours.

Peel apples; cut out core from top of each apple leaving the bottom intact. Combine brown sugar and apple pie spice in a small bowl; mix well. Add melted butter and pecans; mix well. Press mixture into hollows of apples.

Heat oven to 350 degrees. Working with one pastry disc at a time, roll pastry out on a floured surface, forming a 14-inch square. Cut pastry into four 7-inch squares. Place one apple in center of each square; bring up four edges over apple and pinch and twist ends to seal. Place on a parchment- or foil-lined jelly roll pan. Repeat with remaining pastry and apples. Combine egg yolks and remaining 2 tablespoons cream; mix well. Brush mixture lightly over apple dumplings. Bake 50 to 55 minutes or until golden brown and apples are tender when pierced with a skewer. Serve warm or at room temperature with ice cream and caramel topping.

*Makes 8 servings*

# Luau

Mai Tai Punch

Papaya Daiquiris

Tropical Fruit Salad

Grilled Sweet Potato and Onion Packets

Sautéed Spinach

Grilled Duck Quarters with Braised Sweet Onions

Polynesian Duck Kabobs

Nutty Pie Bars

Double Coconut Parfaits

*Wine:* GERMAN RIESLING, SUCH AS DR. LOOSEN "DR. L" RIESLING

The combination of tropical fruits and duck just begs for a juicy, off-dry riesling. German riesling has a vibrant acidity that gives the wines balance and an affinity for sweet-and-sour elements found in this recipe.

# Mai Tai Punch

1½ cups light rum

1 cup orange juice

1 cup pineapple juice

½ cup grenadine syrup

¼ cup Rose's lime juice

¼ cup curaçao or Triple Sec

¼ cup dark rum (optional)

3 cups club soda

Orange, lemon or lime slices

Maraschino cherries

In a large pitcher, combine light rum, orange juice, pineapple juice, grenadine syrup, lime juice, curaçao and, if desired, dark rum; mix well. Chill at least 2 hours or up to 24 hours.

Just before serving, tilt pitcher and slowly pour in club soda; stir. Fill glasses with ice cubes; pour punch over ice and garnish with orange slices and cherries.

*Makes 8 servings*

# Papaya Daiquiris

1 large ripe papaya, peeled, diced or

   2½ cups diced bottled papaya spears

1 cup light rum

1 cup sweet-and-sour cocktail mix

3 tablespoons sugar

8 to 10 ice cubes

Ginger ale (optional)

Small paper umbrellas (optional)

Combine papaya, rum, cocktail mix and sugar in a blender; process until smooth. Add 8 ice cubes; blend until very thick, adding additional ice cubes if a thicker beverage is desired. Pour into martini glasses or wine glasses or serve over ice with a splash of ginger ale. Garnish with opened umbrellas, if desired.

*Makes 8 servings*

*A Turducken is a Cajun dish consisting of a semiboneless or boneless whole turkey stuffed with a boneless whole duck that's stuffed with a boneless whole chicken with layers of corn bread stuffing between each bird.*

Luau

# Tropical Fruit Salad

4 ripe kiwifruit, peeled, sliced

2 ripe papayas, peeled, seeded,
   cut into chunks, divided

$1/2$ large honeydew melon, peeled,
   cut into chunks

1 ripe mango, peeled, seeded,
   cut into chunks

$1/3$ cup honey

3 tablespoons fresh lime juice

2 tablespoons chopped fresh mint leaves

Mint sprigs

In a large bowl, combine kiwifruit, papayas, honeydew melon and mango. In a small bowl, combine honey, lime juice and chopped mint. Pour mixture over fruit; toss well. Serve immediately or cover and chill up to 2 hours before serving. Garnish with mint sprigs.

*Makes 8 servings*

71

## Grilled Sweet Potato and Onion Packets

| | |
|---|---|
| 4 medium sweet potatoes, peeled, sliced $1/4$ inch thick | 1 teaspoon salt |
| | Heavy aluminum foil |
| 1 large Vidalia or other sweet onion, thinly sliced | $1/4$ cup butter, softened |
| | 2 tablespoons brown sugar |
| | $1/8$ teaspoon nutmeg |
| 2 tablespoons canola or vegetable oil | $1/2$ cup chopped salted macadamia nuts, toasted |

Prepare charcoal or gas grill. Combine sweet potatoes and onion rings in a large bowl. Add oil and salt; toss until vegetables are lightly coated with oil.

Tear four sheets of heavy aluminum foil to measure 16×12 inches each. Spoon half of vegetables over center of one sheet of foil; top with another sheet of foil, folding and crimping edges all around sides of foil to form a packet. Repeat with remaining vegetables, forming another packet. Place packets on grid of barbecue grill. Grill, covered, over medium coals (or bake in a 375-degree oven) for 30 to 35 minutes or until sweet potatoes are fork-tender.

Meanwhile, combine butter, brown sugar and nutmeg in a bowl; mix well. Add nuts; mix well. Transfer vegetables to serving plates; top with butter mixture.

*Makes 8 servings*

## Sautéed Spinach

2 pounds fresh spinach
2 tablespoons olive oil
2 teaspoons minced garlic
Salt and freshly ground black pepper
1 tablespoon balsamic vinegar

Wash spinach in cold water; discard tough stems. Drain, but do not dry, spinach. Heat oil in a large saucepan or Dutch oven over medium heat. Add garlic; cook 2 minutes, stirring occasionally. Add spinach to saucepan; cover and cook 3 minutes or until spinach begins to wilt. Uncover; add salt and pepper and vinegar. Toss spinach well. Cover; continue to cook 2 minutes or until all of the spinach is wilted.

*Makes 8 servings*

Luau

# Grilled Duck Quarters with Braised Sweet Onions

8 (12-ounce) Maple Leaf Farms Duck
   Leg Quarters, thawed if frozen
4 medium (about 3 inches in diameter)
   Vidalia or sweet onions, peeled, halved
   crosswise
Cooking spray or olive oil
Duck stock or chicken stock or broth
Salt and freshly ground black pepper
$1/2$ cup soy sauce
$1/4$ cup packed light brown sugar
2 tablespoons seasoned rice vinegar
2 teaspoons minced garlic
2 teaspoons minced gingerroot
$1/4$ teaspoon crushed red pepper flakes

Heat oven to 350 degrees. Place duck in a roasting pan large enough to hold the duck in a single layer. Heat a large cast-iron or heavy nonstick skillet over high heat until very hot. Coat cut sides of onions with cooking spray or brush with olive oil. Place onion halves, cut sides down, in the hot skillet (in batches if necessary). Cook on one side until onions are well browned, about 3 minutes. Arrange browned onions around or over duck. Pour enough stock into roasting pan to come one-third the way up sides of duck. Cover pan with heavy aluminum foil. Place in oven; bake $1^1/2$ to $1^3/4$ hours or until internal temperature of duck reaches 180 degrees.

Transfer duck and onions to separate plates. Sprinkle salt and pepper to taste over onions. Transfer juices from roasting pan to a bowl; cover and refrigerate or freeze for another use. At this point, duck and onions may be covered and refrigerated up to 24 hours before grilling.

Prepare charcoal or gas grill. Combine soy sauce, brown sugar, vinegar, garlic, ginger and pepper flakes in a bowl; mix well. Arrange duck on grid over medium coals; brush about one quarter of soy sauce mixture over duck. Grill, covered, 5 minutes (7 minutes if duck has been refrigerated). Turn; brush another quarter of soy sauce mixture over duck. Continue grilling, covered, 5 to 7 minutes or until duck is well browned. Serve onions at room temperature, or if refrigerated, reheat them in a microwave oven just until warm. Bring remaining soy sauce mixture to a boil; serve with grilled duck and onions.

*Makes 8 servings*

# Polynesian Duck Kabobs

8 (5-ounce) Maple Leaf Farms Skinless,
   Boneless Duck Breast Filets, thawed
   if frozen
Salt and freshly ground black pepper
1 ripe fresh pineapple, peeled, cored
2 large red or yellow bell peppers or
   one of each
2 large green bell peppers
2 small red onions
$2/3$ cup pineapple preserves
3 tablespoons Dijon mustard

*By properly cooking duck, you can eliminate 70 percent of the fat, which leaves a delicious, crisp skin that adds to the distinct flavor of the meat.*

Prepare charcoal or gas grill. Cut duck breast into 2-inch chunks; season with salt and pepper to taste. Cut pineapple into 1$1/2$-inch chunks. Cut bell peppers into 1$1/2$-inch chunks, discarding stems and seeds. Cut onions through the core into $1/2$-inch-thick wedges. Alternately thread duck, pineapple, bell peppers and onions onto large metal skewers.

Combine preserves and mustard in a bowl; mix well. Arrange duck kabobs on grid over medium coals. Brush half of preserve mixture over kabobs. Grill, covered, 5 minutes. Turn; brush remaining half of preserve mixture over kabobs. Continue grilling, covered, 5 to 6 minutes or until duck is barely pink in center and peppers are tender-crisp.

*Makes 8 servings*

Luau

# Nutty Pie Bars

1 (8-ounce) tube refrigerated crescent
   dinner rolls
1/2 cup corn syrup
1/2 cup sugar
1 large egg
1/2 cup chopped pecans
1/2 cup slivered almonds
1 tablespoon butter, melted
1/2 teaspoon cinnamon
1/2 teaspoon pure vanilla extract
1/4 teaspoon nutmeg

Heat oven to 375 degrees. Separate crescent roll dough into two long rectangles; place in an ungreased 13×9-inch baking pan. Press dough over bottom and 1/2 inch up sides of pan. Firmly press perforations to seal. Bake 5 minutes.

Meanwhile, combine remaining ingredients in a medium bowl; mix well. Pour over partially baked crust. Return to oven; bake 18 to 22 minutes or until set and golden brown. Transfer to a wire rack; cool completely. Cut into bars.

*Makes 2 dozen bars*

# Double Coconut Parfaits

1 cup apricot preserves
2 ripe mangoes, peeled, seeded, diced
2 pints coconut ice cream or gelato
1 cup shredded coconut, toasted
Whipped cream
Maraschino cherries

Combine preserves and mangoes in a bowl; mix well. Place a small scoop of ice cream in each of eight parfait or wine glasses, pressing down slightly to flatten. Spoon 2 tablespoons mango mixture and 1 tablespoon toasted coconut over each scoop of ice cream. Repeat layering twice with ice cream, mango mixture and coconut. Serve immediately or cover and freeze until serving time. Garnish with whipped cream and cherries.

Note: If coconut ice cream or gelato is not available, soften 2 pints of vanilla ice cream and stir in 2 teaspoons coconut extract. Freeze until firm and proceed as recipe directs.

*Makes 8 servings*

MAPLE LEAF FARMS

# Picnic on the Beach

Roasted Garlic Duck Sandwiches

Duck and Almond Salad Sandwiches

Potato Artichoke Salad

Lemon Bars

---

*Wine:* WASHINGTON STATE SAUVIGNON BLANC, SUCH AS CHATEAU SAINT MICHELLE, COLUMBIA VALLEY

Sauvignon blancs from Washington have a great balance of fruit and herbal notes
that will complement the mustard and herbs used throughout the recipes.

# Roasted Garlic
# Duck Sandwiches

2 (7.5-ounce) Maple Leaf Farms Roasted
    Garlic or Peppercorn Marinated Boneless
    Duck Breast Filets, thawed if frozen
1/4 teaspoon salt
2 tablespoons stone-ground mustard
2 tablespoons mayonnaise
1/2 cup frisée or gourmet salad greens
4 large slices seeded Italian or rustic bread
4 thin slices tomato
1 thin slice red onion, separated into rings

Heat oven to 375 degrees. Score the skin of the duck breast taking care not to puncture the meat (see glossary). Heat an ovenproof skillet over medium heat until hot. Place duck in skillet skin sides down. Sprinkle salt over duck. Cook 8 minutes or until skin is crisp and golden brown. Turn duck; continue cooking 3 minutes. Transfer duck to a plate; carefully pour off drippings from skillet into a jar with a tight-fitting lid. Refrigerate drippings for another use. Return duck to skillet skin sides up; transfer skillet to oven. Bake 8 to 10 minutes or until internal temperature of duck reaches 155 degrees. Transfer duck to carving board and let stand until cooled, 10 to 15 minutes. (Internal temperature of duck will rise to 160 degrees.) Cut duck lengthwise into thin slices.

Combine mustard and mayonnaise in a small bowl. Arrange frisée over two slices of the bread; top with sliced tomatoes. Spread mustard mixture over tomatoes; top with sliced duck and red onion rings. Close sandwiches with remaining bread. Wrap in aluminum foil; refrigerate until serving time.

*Makes 2 servings*

# Duck and Almond Salad
# Sandwiches

1/4 cup mayonnaise
2 tablespoons sour cream
1 tablespoon chopped fresh tarragon
2 teaspoons tarragon vinegar
1/2 teaspoon dry mustard
1/4 teaspoon salt
1/8 teaspoon freshly ground black pepper
1 cup shredded cooked Maple Leaf
    Farms Duck
1/2 cup diced celery
1/3 cup sliced almonds, toasted
1/4 cup golden raisins
4 small croissants (or 2 large)

In a large bowl, combine mayonnaise, sour cream, tarragon, vinegar, dry mustard, salt and pepper, mixing well. Add duck, celery, almonds and raisins, mixing well. Cover and chill until serving time. Split croissants and fill with duck salad.

*Makes 2 servings*

Make something old, new! Just take your favorite recipe and use duck in place of pork, beef, or chicken. Duck's flavor can stand up to any spice, seasoning, or ethnic profile.

# Potato Artichoke Salad

1¼ pounds small or medium red potatoes

⅓ cup extra virgin olive oil

2 tablespoons red wine vinegar

2 tablespoons stone-ground mustard

½ teaspoon salt

⅛ teaspoon ground white pepper

1 (6- to 7-ounce) jar marinated artichoke
   hearts, drained, coarsely chopped

¼ cup thinly sliced green onions with tops

Tarragon sprigs (optional)

Place potatoes in a medium saucepan; cover with cold water. Bring to a boil over high heat. Reduce heat; simmer, uncovered, until potatoes are tender, about 20 minutes for small potatoes or 22 minutes for medium-sized potatoes. Drain potatoes; rinse with cool water and let stand until cool enough to handle.

Meanwhile, in a large bowl, combine oil, vinegar, mustard, salt and pepper; mix well. Add artichoke hearts and green onions. Cut potatoes into ¼-inch-thick slices; add to bowl and toss lightly to coat. Cover; chill at least 2 hours or up to 24 hours before serving time. Garnish with tarragon sprigs, if desired.

*Makes 4 servings*

# Lemon Bars

1 cup all-purpose flour

1/2 cup unsalted butter, cut into pieces

1/4 cup confectioners' sugar

1/2 teaspoon salt, divided

4 large eggs

1 cup granulated sugar

1/3 cup fresh lemon juice

2 teaspoons grated lemon peel

Sifted confectioners' sugar

Heat oven to 350 degrees. Combine flour, butter, confectioners' sugar and 1/4 teaspoon of the salt in a food processor. Process using on/off pulses until mixture resembles coarse crumbs. Pat dough evenly in an ungreased 9-inch square baking pan. Bake for 20 minutes.

Combine eggs, granulated sugar, lemon juice, lemon peel and remaining 1/4 teaspoon salt in food processor. Process until well combined. When crust has baked 20 minutes, remove pan from oven and pour lemon mixture over hot crust. Return to oven and bake 20 to 22 minutes or until center is set. Transfer pan to wire cooling rack; cool completely. Sprinkle sifted confectioners' sugar over top before cutting into squares. Serve immediately or store, tightly covered, in refrigerator or freezer.

*Makes 16 squares*

# Mountaintop Brunch

Champagne Cocktails

Hint-of-Lemon Blueberry Muffins

Brunch Berry Fruit Salad

Honey Orange Duck Frittata

Duck Hash

Chocolate Pecan Bread Pudding with Bourbon Caramel Sauce

*Wine:* CHILEAN CHARDONNAY, SUCH AS CASA LAPOSTOLLE CHARDONNAY

The citrus and orchard fruit flavors of chardonnay from Chile work nicely with the many flavors of the brunch feast.

# Champagne Cocktails

1/2 cup Grand Marnier, Triple Sec or other
    orange liqueur
1/2 cup orange juice
1/2 cup pineapple juice
1 (750ml) bottle Champagne or sparkling
    white wine, well chilled
6 strawberry halves

Combine Grand Marnier, orange juice and pineapple juice in a large pitcher; stir. Refrigerate at least 30 minutes or up to 8 hours. Just before serving, tilt pitcher and slowly pour Champagne into juice mixture; stir gently. Place strawberry halves in 6 Champagne or wine glasses; add punch.

Nonalcoholic version: Substitute 4 cups ginger ale for the Grand Marnier and Champagne.

*Makes 6 servings*

*White Pekin duck is a breed and should not be confused with Peking duck, which is a popular Chinese preparation of duck.*

# Hint-of-Lemon Blueberry Muffins

MUFFINS

2 cups all-purpose flour

1 tablespoon baking
  powder

1/2 teaspoon salt

2 large eggs

2/3 cup sugar

1 cup half-and-half
  or buttermilk

1 teaspoon grated
  lemon peel

1 teaspoon pure
  vanilla extract

1/2 cup (1 stick) unsalted
  butter, melted
  and cooled

1 cup fresh or frozen
  blueberries

TOPPING

11/2 teaspoons sugar

1/4 teaspoon cinnamon

For muffins, heat oven to 400 degrees. Line a standard 12-muffin pan with paper muffin cups.

In a large bowl, combine flour, baking powder and salt. In a medium bowl, beat together eggs and sugar. Stir in half-and-half, lemon peel and vanilla; add to bowl with flour. Add butter. Mix just until dry ingredients are moistened. Fold in blueberries. Spoon batter into prepared muffin cups.

For topping, combine sugar and cinnamon; sprinkle over batter. Bake 18 to 20 minutes or until muffins are golden brown. Serve warm or at room temperature.

Note: Any extra muffins may be frozen for up to 3 months.

*Makes 12 muffins*

# Brunch Berry Fruit Salad

1/3 cup orange juice

3 tablespoons sugar

1/4 teaspoon pure vanilla extract

2 cups sliced strawberries

2 cups blueberries

2 cups raspberries or blackberries or

   1 cup each

1 cup vanilla or raspberry yogurt

1 tablespoon finely shredded orange peel

In a large bowl, combine orange juice, sugar and vanilla; mix until sugar dissolves. Add berries; toss well. Cover; chill at least 2 hours or up to 6 hours before serving. Spoon into small dessert bowls; top with yogurt and orange peel.

*Makes 6 servings*

*Most ducks in the market are young, tender ducks. A duck called a "mature" will be tougher and will require a longer, tenderizing cooking method like braising or stewing.*

# Honey Orange Duck Frittata

2 (7.5-ounce) Maple Leaf Farms Honey
  Orange Boneless Duck Breast Filets,
  thawed if frozen
8 large eggs
1/2 cup half-and-half or whole milk
1/2 cup sliced green onions
1/2 teaspoon salt
1/4 teaspoon freshly ground black pepper
1 cup shredded smoked Cheddar or Gouda
  cheese, divided

Heat oven to 375 degrees. Score the skin of the duck breast taking care not to puncture the meat (see glossary). Heat a heavy, large, nonstick ovenproof skillet over medium heat until hot. Place duck in skillet, skin sides down. Cook 8 to 9 minutes or until skin is crisp and golden brown. Turn duck; continue cooking 3 minutes. Transfer duck to a small baking sheet (reserve drippings in skillet). Bake duck 8 to 10 minutes or until internal temperature of duck reaches 155 degrees. Transfer duck to carving board and let stand until cooled, 10 to 15 minutes. (Internal temperature of duck will rise to 160 degrees.) Remove skin from duck. Cut duck into 1/2-inch pieces; set aside.

Meanwhile, preheat broiler. Beat eggs in a large bowl. Beat in half-and-half, green onions, salt and pepper. Stir in duck and 1/2 cup of the cheese. Measure drippings in skillet. If there are less than 2 tablespoons drippings, add duck fat or butter to equal 2 tablespoons. Place skillet over medium-high heat until drippings are hot. Add egg mixture; cook without stirring until eggs start to firm and sides and bottom begin to brown, lifting sides occasionally to let uncooked egg run underneath, 4 to 5 minutes. Sprinkle remaining 1/2 cup cheese over egg mixture; transfer to broiler. Broil 5 to 6 inches from heat source 2 to 3 minutes or until eggs are set and cheese is melted and golden brown. Cut into wedges. Serve warm or at room temperature.

Note: If desired, prepare duck skin cracklings for garnish (see glossary).

*Makes 6 servings*

# Duck Hash

| | |
|---|---|
| 4 (8-ounce) Maple Leaf Farms Duck Leg Confit, thawed if frozen | 1 teaspoon salt |
| | 1/4 teaspoon freshly ground black pepper |
| 2 large baking (russet) potatoes (11/4 to 11/2 pounds) | 6 large eggs |
| | 1/4 cup chopped parsley |
| 1/4 cup butter | Ketchup or hot sauce (optional) |
| 1 large onion, diced | |

Cook duck according to package directions. When cool enough to handle, discard skin and bones and shred duck meat (you should have 2 cups shredded meat).

Meanwhile, place potatoes in a large saucepan; add water to cover. Bring to a boil over high heat. Reduce heat; cover and simmer until potatoes are tender, 25 to 30 minutes. Drain and rinse with cold water. When potatoes are cool enough to handle, peel them and cut into 1/2-inch cubes.

Melt butter in a heavy, large, nonstick skillet or cast-iron skillet over medium-high heat. Add onion; cook 4 to 5 minutes, stirring frequently, until onion is golden brown. Stir in potatoes, salt and pepper; cook 2 minutes. Add shredded duck meat; mix well and press down with spatula to compact. Turn heat to medium; cook without stirring for 10 to 12 minutes or until bottom is golden brown.

Meanwhile, poach or fry eggs to desired doneness. Spoon hash onto serving plates browned sides up; top with eggs and parsley. Serve with ketchup or hot sauce, if desired.

Note: Two tablespoons rendered duck fat may be substituted for 2 tablespoons of the butter, if desired.

*Makes 6 servings*

# Chocolate Pecan Bread Pudding with Bourbon Caramel Sauce

BREAD PUDDING

3/4 cup sugar

1/4 cup butter, melted

4 large eggs

2 cups half-and-half or whole milk

8-ounce loaf French or Italian bread, cubed
   (8 to 10 cups)

4 ounces good quality semisweet chocolate
   candy bar, coarsely chopped

3/4 cup coarsely chopped pecans


BOURBON CARAMEL SAUCE

3/4 cup butterscotch, dulce de leche or
   caramel ice cream topping

2 tablespoons bourbon or whiskey

For pudding, heat oven to 350 degrees. In a large bowl, combine sugar and butter, mixing well. Add eggs; mix well. Gradually stir in half-and-half, mixing well. Add bread cubes, chocolate and pecans; toss until most of liquid is absorbed. Butter a 10-inch quiche dish or shallow casserole dish. Spoon bread mixture into dish. Bake 40 to 45 minutes or until golden brown and center is set. Transfer to wire rack; let stand at least 15 minutes.

For sauce, in a small saucepan, heat the ice cream topping until very hot. Remove from heat and stir in bourbon. Spoon pudding onto dessert plates. Serve warm or at room temperature with sauce.

*Makes 6 servings*

MAPLE LEAF FARMS

# Sunset Cruise

Sicilian Marinated Feta Cheese

Red Pepper Basil Duck Rolls

Ratatouille

Rotisserie Duck with Pasta

Duck Confit with Warm Spinach Salad and Spiced Peaches

Flourless Chocolate Cake with Raspberry Sauce

*Wine:* AMERICAN BLANC DE NOIR SPARKLING WINE, SUCH AS GRUET BLANC DE NOIR FROM NEW MEXICO

Sparkling wine is a natural for boat parties or meals by the shore. A rich blanc de noir has
the requisite aromas and flavors that will enhance these elegant dishes.

# Sicilian Marinated Feta Cheese

1/4 cup extra virgin olive oil

1 tablespoon fresh lemon juice

1/2 teaspoon hot pepper sauce

1/4 teaspoon salt

8 ounces feta cheese, diced

1 cup thinly sliced fennel bulb

1 cup seeded, diced tomato

1/4 cup finely chopped parsley

1/4 cup finely chopped chives

1/4 cup thinly sliced red onion

In a large bowl, combine oil, lemon juice, hot pepper sauce and salt; mix well. Add remaining ingredients to bowl; toss with oil mixture. Cover; refrigerate at least 24 hours before serving.

*Makes 4 servings*

# Red Pepper Basil Duck Rolls

2 (5- to 7-ounce) Maple Leaf Farms Smoked
   Duck Breast Halves

3 tablespoons mayonnaise

1 teaspoon lemon juice

1/2 teaspoon hot pepper sauce

12 thick strips roasted red bell peppers

12 large basil leaves

1/2 cup bean sprouts

12 cocktail or wooden picks

Remove skin and slice each duck breast half lengthwise into 6 thin slices. Combine mayonnaise, lemon juice and hot pepper sauce in a small bowl; spread evenly over one side of each of the 12 slices of duck. Arrange 1 strip of red pepper, 1 basil leaf and a few bean sprouts over each duck slice. Roll up; secure with picks.

*Makes 4 appetizer servings*

*White Pekin duck meat is an excellent source of niacin and selenium. Niacin is essential to energy metabolism and DNA repair, while selenium works as an antioxidant to protect cells from damage that may lead to heart disease, cancer, or other heart problems. Selenium also aids in cell growth and boosts immune function.*

# Ratatouille

1/4 cup extra virgin olive oil, divided

1 cup finely diced unpeeled eggplant

3/4 cup finely diced zucchini

1/2 cup finely diced red bell pepper

1/4 cup finely diced onion

1 clove garlic, minced

1 cup finely diced seeded tomato

Salt and freshly ground black pepper

2 ounces Parmesan cheese, shaved with
   a vegetable peeler

Heat 3 tablespoons of the oil in a large skillet over medium-high heat. Add eggplant and zucchini; cook until vegetables are softened and golden brown, stirring occasionally. Transfer vegetables to a bowl; set aside.

Add remaining 1 tablespoon oil, bell pepper and onion to same skillet; cook over medium heat until vegetables are tender, stirring occasionally. Add garlic; cook 1 minute. Add tomato; cook 5 minutes. Return eggplant mixture to skillet; simmer over low heat 10 minutes, stirring occasionally. Season to taste with salt and pepper. Transfer to serving dishes; top with shaved cheese. Serve warm or at room temperature.

*Makes 4 to 6 servings*

*A vertical roaster is a perfect way
to roast a whole duck. Even the beer can roasters
work well with duck.*

# Rotisserie Duck with Pasta

12 ounces pappardelle or fettuccini pasta, uncooked

2 tablespoons rendered duck drippings or olive oil

8 ounces cremini or baby portobello mushrooms, sliced

4 cloves garlic, minced

1/2 cup dry white wine

2 cups duck stock or chicken stock or broth

2 tablespoons balsamic vinegar

2 cups shredded Maple Leaf Farms Fully Cooked Rotisserie Half or Duck Leg Confit

1 (10-ounce) package frozen artichoke hearts, thawed, quartered

1 cup diced plum tomatoes

2 tablespoons chopped fresh sage leaves

2 tablespoons butter

Sage sprigs

Cook pasta according to package directions. Meanwhile, heat duck drippings in a large, deep skillet over medium heat. Add mushrooms and garlic; sauté 5 minutes. Add wine; cook 2 minutes or until slightly reduced. Add duck stock and vinegar; simmer 10 minutes.

Stir in shredded duck, artichoke hearts and tomatoes; simmer 5 minutes. Remove from heat; stir in sage and butter. Drain pasta; toss with sauce. Garnish with sage sprigs.

*Makes 4 servings*

# Duck Confit with Warm Spinach Salad and Spiced Peaches

2 tablespoons light
   corn syrup

1 large egg white

1 tablespoon butter, melted

1 cup pecan halves

1/4 cup Champagne
   vinegar or white
   wine vinegar

1/4 cup sugar

1 teaspoon pure
   vanilla extract

1/2 teaspoon cinnamon

1/4 teaspoon ground cloves
   or allspice

2 medium peaches,
   peeled, sliced

4 (8-ounce) Maple Leaf
   Farms Duck Leg Confit

1/4 cup olive oil

1 clove garlic, minced

1 1/2 tablespoons
   Champagne vinegar or
   white wine vinegar

1/4 teaspoon salt

1/4 teaspoon freshly ground
   black pepper

4 cups packed baby
   spinach leaves

2 cups mesclun or
   assorted torn
   salad greens

Heat oven to 325 degrees. Combine corn syrup, egg white and butter in a bowl; mix well. Add pecans; toss until evenly coated. Arrange pecans on a foil-lined baking sheet. Bake 20 to 25 minutes or until deep golden brown, stirring once after 15 minutes. Remove from oven; let stand until cooled.

Meanwhile, combine 1/4 cup vinegar, sugar, vanilla, cinnamon and cloves in a medium bowl; mix well. Add peaches, tossing to coat. Let stand at room temperature while preparing duck salad.

Cook duck according to package directions. Heat oil in a small skillet over medium heat. Add garlic; cook 2 minutes. Stir in 1 1/2 tablespoons vinegar, salt and pepper; mix well. Combine spinach and mesclun or salad greens; arrange on four large serving plates. Drizzle warm dressing over greens; top with pecans and arrange drained peaches over salads. Place warm duck over salads.

Note: You may substitute 2 cups thawed frozen unsweetened peaches for the fresh peaches.

*Makes 4 servings*

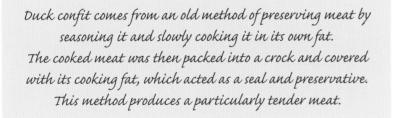

Duck confit comes from an old method of preserving meat by seasoning it and slowly cooking it in its own fat. The cooked meat was then packed into a crock and covered with its cooking fat, which acted as a seal and preservative. This method produces a particularly tender meat.

# Flourless Chocolate Cake with Raspberry Sauce

2 (10-ounce) packages frozen raspberries in
    light syrup, thawed
12 ounces semisweet chocolate bars,
    finely chopped
4 ounces unsweetened chocolate,
    finely chopped
2 cups unsalted butter
1 cup packed light brown sugar
8 large eggs, beaten
Fresh raspberries

For sauce, purée raspberries with their liquid in a food processor. Strain purée; discard seeds. Cover and chill the sauce until serving time.

Heat oven to 350 degrees. Line the bottom of a 9-inch round cake pan with 2-inch sides with parchment paper. Combine semisweet and unsweetened chocolate in a large bowl. In a medium saucepan, combine butter and brown sugar. Bring mixture to a boil, stirring frequently. Pour mixture over chocolate; whisk until chocolate melts. Whisk in eggs.

Pour batter into prepared pan. Place pan in a roasting pan and pour water into roasting pan to come halfway up sides of cake pan. Bake 1 hour or until center is set and wooden pick inserted in center comes out clean. Let cool; cover and chill at least 8 hours or overnight.

Just before serving, use a sharp knife to cut around edges of cake. Place a serving plate over top of cake; invert cake and remove pan and parchment paper. Serve cake with sauce and garnish with fresh raspberries.

*Makes 8 to 10 servings*

# Tailgating

Blue Cheese Dip

Tangy Horseradish Cole Slaw

Double Corn Corn Bread

Duck Chili

Duck Sausage Hoagies

Jumbo Chocolate Chunk Peanut Butter Cookies

---

*Wine:* CALIFORNIA ZINFANDEL, SUCH AS NORMAN VINEYARDS "THE CLASSIC"

You need an all-American wine for a menu like this. The ample fruit and
spiciness of the wine is the perfect match for these tailgate classics.

# Blue Cheese Dip

8 ounces cream cheese, softened

1 cup sour cream

3/4 cup (3 ounces) crumbled blue cheese

2 tablespoons chopped chives

1/2 teaspoon salt

1/4 teaspoon freshly ground black pepper

Dippers: sesame bread sticks,

    potato or pita chips, baby carrots,

    thick slabs of yellow and red bell peppers

In a medium bowl, combine cream cheese and sour cream, mixing well. Stir in blue cheese, chives, salt and pepper. Transfer mixture to a transportable serving dish. Cover and chill until serving time. Pack dippers separately to serve with dip.

Note: Any remaining dip may be thinned with white wine vinegar and served as a salad dressing.

*Makes 12 servings, about 2 1/2 cups dip*

*For an elegant crudité platter, arrange cleaned baby carrots with tops, steamed green beans, and yellow and red cherry tomatoes attractively on a platter.*

Tailgating

# Tangy Horseradish Cole Slaw

1 small head cabbage (2 to 2¼ pounds)

½ cup shredded carrots

¾ cup mayonnaise

½ cup sour cream

¼ cup sugar

¼ cup prepared horseradish

1 tablespoon lemon juice

2 teaspoons spicy brown or hot
   Dijon mustard

¾ teaspoon salt

½ teaspoon celery salt

Core cabbage and cut into chunks. Working in batches, place cabbage in food processor; pulse until finely chopped. Transfer to a very large bowl. (Do not wash food processor.) Add carrots to chopped cabbage. Combine mayonnaise and remaining ingredients in food processor; process until well blended and sugar dissolves. Pour dressing over cabbage mixture; toss well. Cover; chill at least 8 hours or up to 24 hours before serving. Pack in a transportable serving dish; keep chilled in cooler until ready to serve.

*Makes 12 servings, about 8 cups cole slaw*

*Because of the historical connection to Long Island, you will often see packaging on White Pekin ducks proclaiming Long Island Style.*

# Double Corn Corn Bread

2 cups yellow cornmeal

2 cups all-purpose flour

1/2 cup sugar

1 tablespoon baking powder

1 1/2 teaspoons salt

5 large eggs, separated

2 cups buttermilk or half-and-half

1/2 cup butter, melted, cooled

1 cup fresh or thawed frozen corn kernels

Honey butter (optional)

Heat oven to 400 degrees. In a large bowl, combine cornmeal, flour, sugar, baking powder and salt; mix well.

Place egg yolks in a medium bowl. Add buttermilk or half-and-half and set aside. Beat egg whites in a mixing bowl with electric mixer until stiff peaks form. Add egg yolk mixture and butter to dry ingredients, mixing just until dry ingredients are moistened. Lightly fold corn, then beaten egg whites into batter. Pour batter into a greased 13×9-inch baking pan. Bake 22 to 25 minutes or until edges are golden brown and center springs back when touched lightly. Transfer to wire cooling rack; cool completely. Cover tightly with foil. Reheat on grill until warm. Cut into squares. Serve with honey butter, if desired.

Note: For optional honey butter, combine 1/2 cup softened butter with 1/4 cup honey; mix well. Transfer to a plastic transportable container.

*Makes 12 to 16 servings*

Tailgating

# Duck Chili

3 medium onions, cut into
  3/4-inch chunks
8 (12-ounce) Maple Leaf
  Farms Duck Leg
  Quarters, thawed if frozen
1 (12-ounce) bottle beer or
  dark beer
2 cups duck stock or
  double strength chicken
  or beef broth or stock
1 (28-ounce) can diced
  tomatoes, undrained
2 large each red bell
  peppers and green
  bell peppers, cut into
  1-inch chunks
4 large cloves garlic,
  chopped

2 tablespoons chili powder
2 tablespoons
  ground cumin
1 tablespoon hot pepper
  sauce or 1 teaspoon
  cayenne pepper
1 tablespoon dried oregano
2 teaspoons salt
1 (16-ounce) can black
  beans, drained
1 (16-ounce) can red
  kidney beans, drained
Garnishes: sliced or
  chopped jalapeño chile
  peppers, chopped
  cilantro, sour cream,
  shredded Cheddar or
  Monterey Jack cheese

Heat oven to 350 degrees. Place onions in a shallow roasting pan large enough to hold the duck in a single layer. Arrange duck over onions. Pour beer over duck. Pour stock into roasting pan. Cover pan with heavy aluminum foil. Place in oven; bake 1³/4 to 2¹/4 hours or until internal temperature of duck thigh reaches 180 degrees. Cool mixture in pan. Cover and refrigerate at least 4 hours or overnight.

Remove the fat from the top of the duck mixture and reserve for another use. Remove duck from pan. Transfer juices and onions from roasting pan to a Dutch oven or large saucepan. Stir in tomatoes, bell peppers, garlic, chili powder, cumin, hot pepper sauce, oregano and salt. Bring to a boil over high heat. Reduce heat; simmer 25 minutes or until bell peppers are tender.

Meanwhile, discard skin and bones from duck and shred or cut meat into large chunks. Stir duck and beans into chili and simmer 15 minutes longer.

Wrap towels or newspapers around covered pot of chili to keep warm or reheat chili in covered pot on grill. Pack desired garnishes in plastic containers and transport in cooler. Serve alongside chili.

Note: For a thicker chili, partially mash part of the beans before adding to chili and simmer until desired thickness. The chili may be prepared, covered and refrigerated up to 2 days before serving. Leftover chili may be frozen for up to 3 months.

*Makes 12 servings*

# Duck Sausage Hoagies

3 (14-ounce) packages
   Maple Leaf Farms
   Duck Sausage
1 (12-ounce) bottle beer
2 tablespoons butter or
   olive oil
2 large onions, thinly sliced
4 large green bell peppers,
   cut into long, thin strips

2 large red or yellow bell
   peppers, cut into long,
   thin strips
Salt and freshly ground
   black pepper
12 (6-inch) hoagie
   rolls, split
Spicy brown or hot
   Dijon mustard

Place sausages in a large saucepan. Add beer and enough water to barely cover sausages. Bring to a boil over high heat. Reduce heat. Cover and simmer 18 to 20 minutes or until internal temperature of sausages reaches 165 degrees. Drain and cool.

Meanwhile, melt butter in a large, deep skillet over medium-high heat. Add onions and cook 2 minutes. Add bell peppers and cook, stirring frequently, until vegetables are tender and golden brown, about 12 minutes. Remove from heat, season with salt and pepper and let stand until cool.

Place cooled sausages in a plastic portable container and chill until serving time. Wrap cooled vegetables in one or two large foil cooking bags or sheets of heavy aluminum foil, folding envelope fashion. Transport sausages and vegetables in a cooler.

Cook sausages on a grill over medium-high heat, turning occasionally until browned and heated through, 5 to 6 minutes. Place packet(s) of vegetables on side of grill to heat through, turning once. Grill hoagie rolls, cut sides down, until lightly toasted, 1 to 2 minutes. Serve sausages in rolls topped with vegetables and mustard.

*Makes 12 servings*

# Jumbo Chocolate Chunk Peanut Butter Cookies

2¹/₂ cups all-purpose flour

1 teaspoon baking powder

1 teaspoon baking soda

1 teaspoon salt

1 cup butter, softened

1 cup granulated sugar

1 cup packed light
  brown sugar

1 cup plain or chunky
  peanut butter

2 large eggs

2 teaspoons pure
  vanilla extract

2 cups semisweet
  chocolate chunks
  (12-ounce package)

1 cup coarsely chopped
  peanuts (optional)

Heat oven to 350 degrees. In a medium bowl, combine flour, baking powder, baking soda and salt; mix well.

In large bowl of electric mixer, beat butter at medium speed until light and fluffy. Gradually beat in granulated sugar. Beat in brown sugar. Beat in peanut butter, then one egg at a time and vanilla until well combined. On low speed, gradually beat in flour mixture. Beat in chocolate chunks, and, if desired, peanuts.

Measure out ¹/₄ cupfuls of dough using a medium-sized ice cream scoop or a metal ¹/₄ cup measuring cup and place 2 inches apart on ungreased cookie sheets. Flatten each mound of dough to ¹/₂-inch thickness. Bake 14 to 16 minutes or until edges of cookies are golden brown. Let stand on cookie sheets 2 minutes. Transfer to wire cooling rack and cool completely. Store in an airtight container up to 2 days at room temperature. (Cookies may be frozen up to 6 weeks.)

*Makes about 2 dozen cookies*

*Duck eggs have more albumen (the protein in the white) than chicken eggs, which gives them more structure when cooked. For this reason, many people prefer duck eggs for baking. The extra protein creates additional loft.*

105

MAPLE LEAF FARMS

# Thanksgiving

New England Autumn Salad

Green Beans in Roasted Garlic Butter

Baked Sweet Potatoes with Spiced Butter Pecan Topping

Savory Sage Corn Bread Stuffing

Cranberry Pear Relish

Crispy Roast Duck with Giblet Gravy

Roast Duck with Cranberry Orange Sauce

Bourbon Chocolate Pecan Pie

*Wine:* OREGON PINOT NOIR, SUCH AS KING ESTATE PINOT NOIR

The myriad of flavors found on the Thanksgiving table can be a daunting challenge for wine pairing.
But Oregon pinot just blends in so perfectly it seems like it was made just for this occasion.

# New England Autumn Salad

3 tablespoons cider vinegar

1 teaspoon sugar

1 teaspoon finely shredded orange peel

1/2 teaspoon salt

1/4 teaspoon cinnamon

1/3 cup extra virgin olive oil

12 cups packed mesclun or mixed
   salad greens

2 medium oranges or blood oranges,
   peeled, sectioned

2 ripe avocados, peeled, seeded and diced

1 cup coarsely chopped walnuts, toasted

1/2 cup dried cranberries

*Duck cracklings can be easily made by cutting duck skin into thin strips and frying them until they are crisp. They are great on duck dishes or salads.*

Combine vinegar, sugar, orange peel, salt and cinnamon in a small bowl. Gradually whisk in oil until well combined. Cover and chill at least 30 minutes or up to 2 days before serving.

Combine mesclun or salad greens, orange sections, avocados, walnuts and cranberries in a very large bowl. Add half of dressing; toss well and arrange on serving plates. Pass remaining dressing.

Note: Use a sharp chef's knife to cut away all peel from orange, then cut between membranes to form skinless sections of orange.

*Makes 8 servings*

# Green Beans in Roasted Garlic Butter

1 whole head garlic

1¹/2 pounds fresh green beans

¹/3 cup butter

³/4 teaspoon salt

¹/4 teaspoon freshly ground black pepper

Heat oven or toaster oven to 375 degrees. Discard any excess papery skin from garlic head. Wrap the whole unpeeled head of garlic tightly in foil. Bake for 50 to 55 minutes or until garlic is very soft. Open foil and let stand until cool enough to handle. Cut head crosswise in half and squeeze out softened garlic into a small bowl.

Meanwhile, cover green beans with cold water in a large saucepan. Bring to a simmer over high heat. Reduce heat; simmer, uncovered, until beans are tender-crisp, 6 to 8 minutes. Pour into a colander and drain well. Add butter to same saucepan. Add garlic purée and cook over medium heat until butter is melted, mashing garlic with back of a wooden spoon. Return green beans to saucepan. Add salt and pepper. Toss well and cook until beans are hot.

Note: Green beans may be prepared up to two hours before serving and transferred to a covered microwave-safe casserole dish. Reheat in microwave oven just before serving.

*Makes 8 servings*

# Baked Sweet Potatoes with Spiced Butter Pecan Topping

8 large sweet potatoes, scrubbed

1/2 cup unsalted butter, softened

1/4 cup packed light brown sugar

1/2 teaspoon salt

1/2 teaspoon cinnamon

1/3 cup chopped pecans, toasted

Heat oven to 375 degrees. Place potatoes on a baking sheet; bake until very tender, 50 minutes to 1 hour or in a microwave oven on paper towels at high power 12 to 14 minutes, turning potatoes over after 6 minutes.

Meanwhile, combine butter, brown sugar, salt and cinnamon in a small bowl; mix well. Stir in pecans. Split open hot sweet potatoes; serve with topping.

*Makes 8 servings*

# Savory Sage Corn Bread Stuffing

1/2 cup unsalted butter

1 large onion, chopped

1/2 cup thinly sliced celery

3 tablespoons chopped fresh sage

2 1/2 cups duck stock or chicken broth

6 cups packaged corn bread stuffing mix

Heat oven to 375 degrees. Melt butter in a large saucepan over medium heat. Add onion, celery and sage; cook 5 minutes, stirring occasionally. Add stock or broth; bring to a boil. Remove from heat; stir in stuffing mix until moistened. Transfer to a buttered casserole dish. Cover; bake 25 to 30 minutes or until stuffing is hot.

*Makes 8 servings*

*Duck fat, which is low in saturated fat, is excellent to sauté vegetables, fry foods, or make omelets. It has a high smoke point and adds a great flavor.*

# Cranberry Pear Relish

1 (12-ounce) package fresh cranberries

1 cup packed light brown sugar

1/2 cup apple juice

1 teaspoon ground ginger

1 teaspoon cinnamon

2 large ripe but firm Bartlett or Comice
    pears, peeled, diced

Combine cranberries, brown sugar, apple juice, ginger and cinnamon in a heavy medium saucepan. Bring to a boil over high heat, stirring often. Reduce heat; simmer, uncovered, 10 minutes or until berries are popped and sauce thickens. Stir in pears; simmer 3 minutes or just until pears are tender. Remove from heat; let cool. Cover; refrigerate at least 4 hours or up to 2 days before serving.

Store any leftover relish in the refrigerator for up to 1 week. Spoon over a brick of softened cream cheese and serve with crackers for a quick appetizer or snack.

*Makes 8 servings, about 4 cups relish*

*When a roasted whole duck has completed cooking, the legs will wiggle easily.*

# Crispy Roast Duck with Giblet Gravy

2 (5-pound) Maple Leaf
   Farms Ducks, thawed
   if frozen
2 cups chicken broth
1 cup water
1 onion unpeeled,
   quartered
2 large carrots, cut into
   1/2-inch chunks
2 small sprigs fresh sage
1 large bay leaf

1 teaspoon dried
   thyme leaves
1/2 teaspoon black
   peppercorns
3/4 cup dry vermouth or
   dry white wine
1/4 cup all-purpose flour
Salt and freshly ground
   black pepper
Sage sprigs (optional)

Remove giblets and orange sauce packets from ducks and reserve for another use. Rinse ducks; pat dry with paper towels. Place breast sides up on a rack in a large, shallow roasting pan. Roast according to package directions.

Place duck giblets and necks in a large saucepan. Add broth, water, onion, carrots, sage sprigs, bay leaf, thyme and peppercorns. Bring to a boil over high heat. Reduce heat; simmer gently, uncovered, 1 hour. Strain broth; set aside giblets and discard remaining solids. If broth measures less than 2 cups, add water to equal 2 cups.

Remove roast ducks from oven and transfer to rack of broiler pan. Preheat broiler. Pour off and reserve the drippings from the roasting pan. Add vermouth to pan and cook over medium-high heat, stirring constantly with a wooden spoon, until the mixture is reduced by about half, 2 to 3 minutes.

Spoon off 1/4 cup fat from reserved drippings and reserve any remaining fat for another use; transfer to a medium saucepan. Add flour; cook, stirring constantly, over medium heat 1 minute. Add 2 cups duck broth and the wine mixture to saucepan. Add drippings to saucepan. Cook, stirring frequently, until gravy thickens. Chop reserved giblets and add to gravy. Simmer 3 minutes. Season to taste with salt and pepper.

Broil ducks 5 to 6 inches from heat source until skin is well browned and crispy, 6 to 8 minutes. Cut each duck into quarters and transfer to serving plates. Pass gravy separately. Garnish with sage sprigs, if desired.

*Makes 8 servings*

# Roast Duck with Cranberry Orange Sauce

4 (12-ounce) Maple Leaf Farms Fully Cooked

    Rotisserie Duck Halves, thawed if frozen

2 tablespoons butter

1/2 cup chopped shallots or sweet onion

1 tablespoon all-purpose flour

1/2 cup duck stock or chicken broth

1/2 cup orange juice

1 cup whole cranberry sauce or

    cranberry chutney

1/2 teaspoon finely shredded orange peel

1/4 teaspoon salt

Heat oven to 375 degrees. Remove duck halves from packaging and place in a shallow roasting pan. Bake 25 minutes or until heated through.

Meanwhile, melt butter in a heavy medium saucepan over medium heat. Add shallots; cook 5 minutes, stirring occasionally. Add flour; cook 1 minute. Add stock and orange juice; simmer, stirring frequently, until sauce thickens, about 3 minutes. Stir in cranberry sauce or chutney, orange peel and salt; heat through. Divide each duck half into two portions; transfer to serving plates and serve with sauce.

*Makes 8 servings*

# Bourbon Chocolate Pecan Pie

Pastry for a 9-inch pie plate

3 large eggs

1 cup packed light brown sugar

1 cup light corn syrup

1/4 cup butter, melted, cooled

2 tablespoons bourbon or whiskey

2 teaspoons pure vanilla extract

1/2 teaspoon salt

1 1/2 cups pecan halves or coarsely

    chopped pecans

3/4 cup semisweet chocolate chunks or chips

Sweetened whipped cream

Heat oven to 375 degrees. Line pie plate with pastry; fold edges under and flute attractively.

In a large bowl, beat eggs with brown sugar with a wooden spoon until well combined. Stir in corn syrup, butter, bourbon, vanilla and salt; mix well. Stir in pecans and chocolate chunks. Pour mixture into pastry-lined plate. Bake 40 minutes or until crust is deep golden brown. (Center may appear soft but will set upon cooling.) Transfer pie to a wire cooling rack; let stand at least 1 hour before serving. Serve warm or at room temperature with whipped cream.

*Makes 8 servings*

# Holiday Party

Roast Duck with Peach Nectar Sauce

Whiskey Duck

Risotto with Exotic Mushrooms and Spinach

Orange-Scented Sugar Snap Peas

Cider-Roasted Acorn Squash

Southern Spoon Bread with Spiced Walnuts

Poached Pears in Raspberry Sauce

*Wine:* AUSTRALIAN SHIRAZ, SUCH AS PETER LEHMAN SHIRAZ

These rich, full-flavored dishes work best with a big, full-throttle shiraz. The blackberry, plum, and vanilla flavors of Australian shiraz are a natural with these holiday classics.

# Roast Duck with Peach Nectar Sauce

3 (12-ounce) Maple Leaf Farms Fully Cooked

Rotisserie Duck Halves, thawed if frozen

1 tablespoon rendered duck fat or butter

1/2 cup chopped sweet onion or shallots

2 cloves garlic, minced

1 (11.5-ounce) can peach nectar

2 tablespoons light brown sugar

2 tablespoons cider vinegar

2 tablespoons ketchup or chili sauce

1/4 teaspoon crushed hot red pepper flakes

2 teaspoons cornstarch

1 tablespoon cold water

*Duck should never be defrosted on the counter but instead defrosted in the refrigerator. A breast will thaw overnight, while a whole bird can take two days or more. For faster thawing, submerge duck in original packaging in COLD water, changing water every thirty minutes.*

Heat oven to 375 degrees. Remove duck halves from packaging and place in a shallow roasting pan. Bake 25 minutes or until heated through.

Meanwhile, heat duck fat in a medium saucepan over medium heat. Add onion and garlic; cook 5 minutes, stirring occasionally. Add nectar, brown sugar, vinegar, ketchup and pepper flakes; bring to a simmer. Reduce heat; simmer, uncovered, 10 minutes. Combine cornstarch with 1 tablespoon cold water; mix well. Add to sauce; continue simmering 2 minutes, stirring frequently.

Divide each duck half into two portions; transfer to serving plates and top with sauce.

*Makes 6 servings*

# Whiskey Duck

1/4 cup whiskey or bourbon

2 tablespoons honey

2 tablespoons minced shallot or onion

2 cloves garlic, minced

1 tablespoon chopped fresh thyme

1 tablespoon chopped fresh rosemary

6 (7.5-ounce) Maple Leaf Farms Boneless
   Duck Breast Filets, thawed if frozen

1/2 teaspoon salt

1/2 teaspoon freshly ground black pepper

2 tablespoons all-purpose flour

1 cup duck stock or chicken broth

Salt and freshly ground black pepper
   (optional)

Thyme or rosemary sprigs

For marinade, in a small bowl, combine whiskey, honey, shallot, garlic, thyme and rosemary; mix well. Place duck breasts in a resealable plastic bag; add marinade to bag. Seal bag; turn over several times to coat duck with marinade. Refrigerate for 2 to 24 hours.

Heat oven to 375 degrees. Remove duck from marinade, reserving marinade. Pat duck dry with a paper towel. Score the skin of the duck breast taking care not to puncture the meat (see glossary). Heat two large skillets over medium heat until hot. Place 3 duck breasts in each skillet skin sides down. Sprinkle 1/2 teaspoon salt and 1/2 teaspoon pepper lightly over meaty sides of duck in skillets. Cook 8 to 9 minutes or until skin is crispy and golden brown. Turn duck; continue cooking 3 minutes. Or, cook in two batches in the same skillet, pouring off and reserving drippings after cooking the first batch. Transfer duck to a baking sheet, skin sides up. Bake 16 to 20 minutes or until internal temperature of duck reaches 155 degrees. Transfer duck to carving board; cover with foil and let stand 5 minutes. (Internal temperature of duck will rise to 160 degrees.)

Carefully pour off all but 2 tablespoons drippings from skillets into a jar with a tight-fitting lid and refrigerate for another use. Add flour to drippings in skillet; cook over medium heat, stirring constantly, 1 minute. Add duck stock and reserved marinade to skillet. Simmer gently 10 minutes. Season with salt and pepper to taste. Carve duck crosswise into thin slices; arrange on warmed serving plates. Spoon sauce over duck. Garnish with thyme or rosemary sprigs.

*Makes 6 servings*

Duck, like all meats and poultry,
should rest after cooking to allow the juices
to settle in the meat.

# Risotto with Exotic Mushrooms and Spinach

4 cups duck stock or
    reduced-sodium
    chicken broth
2 tablespoons butter
2 (4-ounce) packages
    sliced exotic mushrooms
    such as oyster, shiitake
    or cremini
1/2 cup chopped shallots or
    sweet onion

1 1/2 cups arborio or
    short-grain rice
1/2 cup dry white wine or
    dry vermouth
6 ounces baby spinach
    leaves (4 cups packed)
Salt and freshly ground
    black pepper
1 cup freshly grated
    Parmesan cheese,
    divided

Place stock or broth in a medium saucepan; bring to a simmer over high heat. Reduce heat; keep stock at a gentle simmer.

Melt butter in a large, deep skillet over medium-high heat. Add mushrooms and shallots; cook 3 minutes, stirring occasionally. Stir in rice; cook 1 minute. Add wine; cook until wine is absorbed. Add 1 cup broth mixture to skillet. Simmer, stirring frequently, until broth is absorbed. Continue to add broth 1/2 cup at a time, keeping rice mixture at a constant simmer and stirring frequently. Repeat until rice is tender and mixture has a creamy consistency, about 18 minutes. (If necessary, after all of the broth is absorbed, add small amounts of hot water until rice is tender.)

Stir in spinach 1 cup at a time just until wilted. Season to taste with salt and pepper. Stir in half of cheese. Transfer to serving plates; top with remaining cheese.

*Makes 6 servings*

# Orange-Scented Sugar Snap Peas

1 1/2 pounds sugar snap peas

1/4 cup butter

1 teaspoon salt

1/2 teaspoon freshly ground black pepper

2 teaspoons finely shredded orange peel

In a large saucepan, cover sugar snap peas with cold water. Bring to a simmer over high heat. Reduce heat; simmer until tender-crisp, 5 to 6 minutes. Drain well and return to same pan. Add butter, salt and pepper. Cook over medium heat until butter melts, stirring frequently. Transfer to a serving bowl; top with orange peel.

*Makes 6 servings*

# Cider-Roasted Acorn Squash

3 small acorn squash, 2 1/2 to 2 3/4 pounds total

1 cup apple cider or apple juice

1/4 cup packed light brown sugar

1/2 teaspoon cinnamon

1/4 teaspoon salt

1/8 teaspoon ground cloves

2 tablespoons butter, melted

Pomegranate seeds (optional)

Heat oven to 375 degrees. Cut squash crosswise in half. Scoop out and discard seeds. Pour apple cider into a 13×9-inch baking dish. Place squash halves cut sides down in dish, overlapping if necessary. Bake, uncovered, 45 to 55 minutes or until squash is tender when pierced with a sharp knife.

Remove baking dish from oven. Turn squash cut sides up. Combine brown sugar, cinnamon, salt and cloves; sprinkle over squash. Brush butter over squash. Return to oven; bake 5 minutes. Transfer to a serving platter or plates. If there is any cider remaining in dish, drizzle over squash. Garnish with pomegranate seeds, if desired.

*Makes 6 servings*

*Serve a sauce on the plate or on the side with duck. Putting sauce on the crispy skin will make the skin go soft.*

# Southern Spoon Bread with Spiced Walnuts

| SPICED WALNUTS | SPOON BREAD |
|---|---|
| 1 large egg white | 2 cups cold water |
| 1 cup large walnut pieces | 1 cup yellow cornmeal |
| 1/4 cup sugar | 3/4 teaspoon salt |
| 1 tablespoon cinnamon | 3 tablespoons butter, cut |
| 1/8 teaspoon salt | into pieces |
| 1/8 teaspoon ground cloves | 1 cup whole or 2% milk |
| 1/8 teaspoon nutmeg | 3 large eggs, beaten |
| | 1 teaspoon baking soda |

For spiced walnuts, heat oven to 300 degrees. In a small bowl, beat egg white with a fork until frothy. Add the walnuts and toss to coat. In a medium bowl, combine sugar, cinnamon, salt, cloves and nutmeg; mix well. Remove the walnuts from the egg whites and add to the sugar mixture. Toss to coat well with sugar mixture. Arrange in a single layer on a foil-lined baking or cookie sheet. Bake 30 minutes or until golden brown. Immediately transfer walnuts to a sheet of waxed paper; let stand until cool. (Walnuts may be prepared up to 48 hours before serving. Store tightly covered at room temperature.)

For spoon bread, heat oven to 425 degrees. Place water in a heavy medium saucepan. Gradually whisk in cornmeal and salt. Place over high heat; bring to a boil. Reduce heat to low; simmer 5 minutes, whisking occasionally. (Mixture will be thick.) Remove from heat; whisk in butter until melted. Gradually whisk in milk, then eggs and baking soda.

Pour mixture into a buttered 1¹/2-quart soufflé dish or round casserole dish. Bake 25 to 30 minutes or until puffed and golden brown. (Center will be creamy.) Spoon onto serving plates; top with walnuts.

*Makes 6 servings*

# Poached Pears in Raspberry Sauce

1 (750 milliliter) bottle riesling, Rhine or other
    sweet white wine

6 large firm Bosc or Comice pears

3 or 4 cinnamon sticks

5 or 6 whole cloves

2 (10-ounce) packages frozen raspberries
    in syrup, thawed

2 tablespoons brown sugar

2 teaspoons cornstarch

1 tablespoon cold water

1/2 cup semisweet chocolate chips (optional)

Mint sprigs (optional)

Pour wine into a large saucepan. Use an apple corer or small sharp knife to core pears from the bottom up, removing seeds. Peel pears leaving stems intact. As they are peeled, immediately transfer to the saucepan and coat with wine to prevent discoloration. Add cinnamon sticks and cloves. Add enough water to saucepan to barely cover pears. Bring to a simmer over high heat. Reduce heat to medium-low; simmer pears, turning over occasionally, until tender when pierced with a sharp knife, 15 to 20 minutes.

Meanwhile, purée raspberries in a food processor; press mixture through a strainer and discard seeds. Combine purée and brown sugar in a small saucepan. Bring to a boil over high heat. Reduce heat; simmer 5 minutes. Combine cornstarch with 1 tablespoon cold water in a small bowl, mixing well. Stir into raspberry mixture. Continue to simmer 5 minutes or until sauce thickens, stirring frequently. Transfer to a pitcher or measuring cup; cover and refrigerate at least 30 minutes.

Use a slotted spoon to transfer pears to a plate. Cover with plastic wrap and refrigerate. Pears may be refrigerated up to 24 hours before serving. Serve chilled or let stand at room temperature 30 minutes before serving.

To serve, pour raspberry sauce onto 6 dessert plates. Top each with a pear. If desired, place chocolate chips in a small freezer bag; seal bag. Microwave at high power for 30-second intervals until chocolate is melted. Cut off a tiny end of bag; drizzle chocolate decoratively over pear and sauce. Garnish with mint sprigs.

*Makes 6 servings*

# Duck How-tos

To cut up a whole duck, first take the duck from the package and remove giblets and packets from the cavity. Rinse the duck inside and out under cold running water. Pat the duck dry. Place the duck breast side up on a clean, flat, solid cutting surface. Be sure to use a sharp kitchen knife.

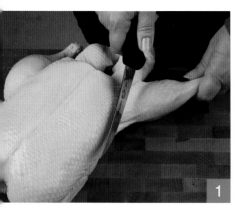
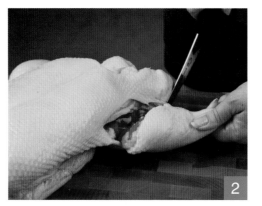

## REMOVE THE LEGS

Pull the whole leg firmly away from the body, putting pressure on the body. Cut through the skin and into the meat where the leg meets the body. Bend the leg back until the ball of the thighbone pops loose. Cut between the ball and the socket to separate the leg. Next, lay the knife flat against the body and cut through the meat to remove the thigh and leg. Repeat with the other leg.

## REMOVE THE BREASTS

Make a shallow incision running along one side of the breast bone. Continue cutting down and around the wishbone. Keep the knife blade flat against the breastbone and ribs and cut the breast from the bones while pulling the breast away with even tension. Be sure to remove the meat attached to the rib cage by keeping the knife flat against it and slicing downward. Slice through the skin and remove the breast. Repeat with the other side.

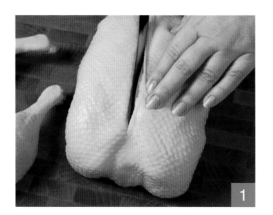

Maple Leaf Farms

## REMOVE THE WINGS

With the duck on its back, remove the wings by cutting inside of the wing just over the joint. Pull wing away from body and cut down through the skin and the joint. Repeat with the other wing.

## PIECES

You now have two leg and thigh pieces, two boneless breasts, and two wings. The remaining carcass, along with the wings, can be used for making stock. The wings do not have a lot of meat on them, but they can be made into hot wings just like chicken wings.

## SCORING DUCK BREASTS

In order to properly cook a boneless duck breast, you need to score the skin. Place the duck breast meat side down. With a sharp knife, draw the blade at a diagonal through the skin, being careful not to cut into the meat. Make cuts at about 1/4- to 1/2-inch intervals. Rotate the breast and score again, making a criss-cross pattern.

Turn the breast over, meat side up, and trim any skin that extends beyond the meat. At this point the duck breast is ready to be used in any recipe. Or, you can season with any preferred seasonings and sauté. Preheat an electric skillet to 325 degrees or a sauté pan on medium-low heat. Place the duck breast skin side down for about 8 to 12 minutes until fat is rendered and skin is golden brown. Turn the breast over and cook 1 to 2 minutes. At this point you can remove it from the heat, place in a sealed container, and refrigerate up to 3 days before finishing in the oven or on a grill.

# Index

Maple Leaf Farms

*I enjoy using Maple Leaf Farms ducks for their consistency, rich flavor, and tenderness. When roasted, they produce a golden crisp skin and sweet tender flesh.*

Bill Cardwell — *Chef/Owner*
Cardwells At The Plaza, *Frontenac, Missouri*

*After several years of working with Maple Leaf Farms duck breasts and duck leg confit, I can honestly say that I have never seen such a consistent product in regard to size, flavor, and appearance. Working in a restaurant that has such a high standard for food quality and consistency, Maple Leaf Farms products have been a blessing. I know that I can always count on it being the same every time. A big thanks to all of the people that have such a dedication to supplying the best product possible.*

Christopher Johnson — *Dinner Sous Chef*
Kincaids Fish, Chop and Steakhouse, *Bloomington, Minnesota*

*I use Maple Leaf Farms smoked duck breast, because it is consistently delicious, and it's convenient when I need to crank out 100 Smoked Duck Quesadillas with Tequila Crème Fraîche for a banquet. I've been cooking Maple Leaf Farms duck breast exclusively since 2001.*

Dan McEachern — *Executive Chef*
Dosey Doe Coffeehouse, *The Woodlands, Texas*

*We love to offer Maple Leaf Farms duck. Offering duck breast with Gorgonzola as an appetizer gives our guests the opportunity to experience the fantastic quality without committing to an entire entrée. The next question they have is, "Why don't you offer this as an entrée?" We like to make them ask.*

Rich LoRusso — *Chef/Owner*
LoRusso's Cucina, *St. Louis, Missouri*

128